Beyond Fear
Growing into faith

Jennifer Minney

with illustrations by
Brian Minney

Silvertree Publishing

Published 2001
by
Silvertree Publishing
PO Box 2768, Yeovil, Somerset

ISBN: 0-9538446-5-X

A catalogue record for this book is available from the
British Library

Printed and bound by
Bookcraft, Midsomer Norton

Author's Note

For the sake of clarity, the masculine pronoun "he" has been used throughout the book, although the text is equally, and in some cases more, applicable to women.

Contents

1

INTRODUCTION AND OVERVIEW

NORMAL FEAR

Definition of Fear

The word fear derives from the old English, "faer", which is the feeling evoked by sudden calamity or danger. Nowadays, the word is used to cover a range of emotions, like apprehension, nervousness, terror, dread.... But, in its true sense, fear is an appropriate and helpful response to an alarming person or situation. This is in contrast to anxiety, which comes from the Latin, "anxietus", meaning troubled in mind about some uncertain event. Since anxiety does not have a specific object it tends to be chronic and ineffectual, and for this reason is not generally classed as normal. Other abnormal fears include timidity, which is a tendency to be easily frightened; phobia, which is excessive fear of a specific stimulus; and panic, which is uncontrollable fear.

Whether the emotion felt is a mild sense of misgiving or abject terror, fear can be described as normal and healthy when it is a reaction to any kind of threat or danger, when the feeling is in proportion to the perceived menace, and when the fear triggers just enough stress to either deal with the situation or run from it. For instance, the surge of adrenalin caused by fear can give us the speed necessary to escape a would-be mugger, avoid an oncoming car or run from a flood or avalanche. Similarly, the nervousness felt before giving a speech or taking part in a race can enhance performance, and a small amount of trepidation enables us to cope better with adverse circumstances, like taking exams or facing painful treatment or surgery. But excessive or inappropriate fear gets in the way, hindering our ability to cope – as does too little fear. People who cannot feel fear never learn to avoid danger, so they keep getting hurt.

And when they go so far as to deny those normal fears that we are born with, they also hinder the development of a healthy, instinctive knowledge of danger.

Innate Fear

Right from birth, babies react with fear to sudden loud noises or any unexpected movement. This startle reflex is most noticeable if the baby feels it is going to be dropped. Crawling infants show a marked fear of falling from a height, and between the ages of six and twelve months most infants develop a fear of strangers; specifically of unfamiliar faces and masks. This is demonstrated in very obvious avoidance behaviour, like clinging to mother, crying or hiding. As this fear develops regardless of the baby's circumstances it is presumed to be innate, even though it is not manifested until some time after birth.

We seem also to have an in-born propensity to fear certain things. For instance, we are far more likely to fear animate rather than inanimate objects, especially snakes and spiders. And the alarm is usually triggered by the creature's jerky or wriggling movements, as opposed to its general appearance. Between the ages of two and three, many children go through a phase of being uneasy around animals, domestic and otherwise, and they will recoil from stroking or petting them. And long after they have outgrown this fear, they will approach all animals with caution.

All of these innate fears, which revolve around threats from people or animals and environmental dangers, were undoubtedly protective in earlier generations. And, to some extent, they continue to be so today. The same applies to many of the fears that, as children, we learned from our elders.

Learned Fear

We begin learning fear even before birth, through experiencing and sensing our mother's fears. And as small babies we discern fear in those closest to us and internalise it, so that the feeling becomes our own. Later, we learn to be afraid because of verbal warnings of danger, often with augmented gestures and facial expressions; or through witnessing fearful reactions in others. For example, if a child sees an older brother backing off from a vicious dog, the child will also feel anxious and model his behaviour on his brother's. In addition, we learn fear through personal experience: being bitten by a dog, burned on a hot stove, abused by an angry parent.... In all these cases, the fear is a normal one, however unnatural the cause.

Fear may also develop because of one's own imagination and this occurs especially around the ages of four to six. During this period, children are often afraid of the dark because of the imaginary creatures, such as ghosts, bogeymen, devils or dinosaurs, who may be lurking there. Other common fears in childhood may have a basis in reality, but are rendered more threatening by mental imagery. These include staring eyes, thunderstorms or fast-moving objects, like cars or trains. Between the ages of six and ten, children's fears can be very intense and overpowering, so they often develop little rituals to protect themselves. However, these childish terrors seldom persist.

As adults we are confronted with new fears, although these are often variations of those we were born with, or learned in infancy. For example, the fear of heights is thought to be linked with the innate fear of falling, and stage fright connected with the baby's fear of strange faces and staring eyes. Other common fears learned in adult life include driving, facing exams, dental or medical treatment, or combat. Since all of these are potentially dangerous, the fears, in moderation, are normal – as is the universal fear of death. This is common in most cultures and seems to be not so much a dread of dying, but of being cut off too soon, with one's dreams and ambitions still unfulfilled.

As in childhood, adult fears can be learned by witnessing fear in others, through personal experience of danger, or because of one's own imagination. But in this modern age we also learn fear through exposure to potentially frightening situations that did not exist in previous generations, or that wouldn't be known about. In a sense, the fear evoked by disturbing news items, horror movies and the like is normal in that it is expected and reasonable and in proportion to the cause. Its aberrance lies in its excess.

If you are prone to fear, it will help if you begin by accepting fear as a fact of life, identifying those fears in yourself that are normal and potentially useful. It is not weak or sinful, or an indication of lack of faith to be afraid. You may also find it constructive to look back over your own childhood, to discover how and why your own particular fears arose. If you consider them to be excessive or irrational, and you have blamed yourself for letting your feelings get out of control, then also start taking into account the disturbing fact that nowadays there is more reason to be afraid.

EXCESSIVE FEAR

New Personal Dangers

The changes that occurred during the nineteenth and twentieth centuries have greatly intensified the risk of personal danger, in part because of urbanisation. Living in a city can have its advantages, but there is an increased possibility of being a victim of violence or crime, or of being involved in a road accident. Faster and more extensive travel and the escalation of car ownership have likewise exposed us to greater perils, as well as creating new anxieties revolving around delays and the need to meet connections. There is also more likelihood of having to contend with people who are unpredictable, irate, or even dangerous.

Another result of urbanisation and increased travel, with subsequent greater intermingling, is a more pervasive fear of nationwide epidemics, like meningitis or BSE. While there have always been devastating plagues and life-threatening infections, they can now occur on a much grander scale, and there is nowhere to hide. Country folk are no more immune than city dwellers, and there our interconnectedness also puts animals at greater risk of succumbing to uncontained viral infections, like foot and mouth. The possibility of farmers losing their livelihood through epidemics is increased by today's escalating bureaucracy, with all its red tape and tighter control by faceless directors in increasingly larger organisations. On all fronts, then, there is a feeling of being out of control, which means that fear itself has become endemic.

Whether one lives in the town or country, the loss of control over one's own life, together with today's throwaway mentality, has led to a more subtle and malignant cause of fear: the erosion of one's identity. Nowadays, people tend to feel that they are merely cogs in a machine, and so can easily be dispensed with. Individual abilities and craftsmanship are no longer valued as they were in former generations. Instead, there is added pressure to achieve academic success, with a corresponding fear of failure. Apart from the practical threats of redundancy and unemployment, this dehumanisation creates an inner disquiet: a vague fear of becoming invisible, or even of disappearing.

The fear of losing one's personal identity is exacerbated by the devaluation of the Judaeo-Christian ethics that have stood firm for millennia. Now, as never before, people are questioning their own values; they no longer know what they believe or think, or what is important. There are also new fears around family issues. For instance, marriage is no longer expected to be "until death us do part", so there is a more pervasive fear of divorce, and the worry of having to raise children single-handed. Added to this, the constantly changing views about how one should discipline – or not discipline – children means that parents are becoming increasingly anxious about their parenting abilities. And there is a greater fear of losing control as children become more disruptive and unmanageable. To make matters worse, the erosion of Christian standards in the name of care and sensitivity is giving rise to confusion and guilt, which naturally create a sense of unease. These social changes are especially frightening because they are occurring on a global scale.

New Global Threats

The term, "global village", has been coined to describe a world that has shrunk as a result of faster and more frequent travel and the rapid exchange of information. Events taking place in one country have as much impact on other nations as, formerly, a happening in one village street affected residents living on the other side of the green. The result is an explosion of fear due to such things as oil spills, radiation leaks, food contamination, epidemics and war. And although sexual and racial discrimination

11

have always existed, the greater mingling of nationalities and cultures means that there is more exposure to physical and emotional intimidation on the grounds of gender or skin colour.

As well as being affected by people and events we would normally know nothing about, our global village life increases the likelihood of our being impinged upon by decisions made overseas, by politicians, national leaders, directors of organisations and the like. And these decisions often aim at homogenisation: trying to make everyone the same. This is, in part, because of the difficulty adjusting to our rapidly changing world and being overwhelmed by the enormity and complexity of racial and ethnic differences. So, there is an erosion of national as well as personal identity, with a corresponding feeling of helplessness that is naturally very worrying. This disintegration of cultural values is accompanied by what has been termed anomie: lack of the usual social or ethical standards in an individual or group. And this in turn gives rise to frightening feelings of disorientation and bewilderment, especially as we are also repeatedly bombarded with contradictory information from a wide variety of sources.

New Awareness of Danger

Today, as never before, we are constantly exposed to fear through the media and internet. Newspapers especially tend to focus on negative events, and on their most disturbing and alarming aspects, in order to grab the readers' attention. Then, every detail is reported for weeks on end, and avidly pursued by the very readers it disturbed and frightened in the first place. The compulsion to keep reading about a frightening event comes in part from an unconscious need to know, therefore to be in control. But when the event is not directly connected with one's own life and circumstances, the opposite happens, and a downward spiral ensues. For instance, a newspaper report of abuse produces fear, which creates a need to be acquainted with all the details of the abuse; the acquired knowledge leads to yet more fear, which in turn creates an even greater need to know. The end result is that we become excessively and unrealistically afraid: every teenage boy becomes a possible mugger, every man who enjoys teaching children football is thought to be a paedophile, and every woman who hugs a hurt child in the street is suspected of being a sexual offender.

Not only do we constantly read and hear about crime, we are also informed on a daily – even hourly – basis about food scares, life-threatening epidemics, environmental disasters, racial unrest, political tension, and the threat of nuclear war. We are also bombarded with frightening images through such things as crime stories and horror movies. In all these instances the fear itself may be normal, being in proportion to the cause: it is the proliferation of frightening situations, and our exposure to them, that is unreasonable and harmful.

As you become increasingly aware of how you have been affected by your environment, you will be able to take steps to eliminate at least some of the causes of fear. This will immediately reduce your general anxiety level, enabling you to look more clearly at any irrational fears and identify the form they take. Abnormal fears can be divided into four main groups: free-floating anxiety, timidity, phobia and panic. But these are not four distinct types of fear; they merge and overlap.

UNHEALTHY FEAR

Free-floating Anxiety

The second-most common emotional problem, following depression, is free-floating anxiety. The term, "free-floating", is prefixed to indicate that "anxiety" is used in its original sense, to describe a troubled feeling that exists even when there is no recognisable danger. This has become necessary because nowadays the word anxiety is also used to denote a vague fear of an actual forthcoming event, such as an exam. In this case, some anxiety is normal, as evinced by its dissipating once the danger is past. Free-floating anxiety, on the other hand, tends to persist, whatever the circumstances. It is akin to worry and often occurs in conjunction with depression.

Free-floating anxiety is found more or less equally in men and women, of all types, nationalities, cultures or religion. It tends to start in young adulthood, but can strike at any age. However, although anxiety is the same the world over, one's cultural and religious beliefs do affect the way it is manifested. Occasionally, epidemics of anxiety can sweep through an entire community, having been triggered by a scare of some kind. These rarely have any lasting effect, but when anxiety is allowed to take hold, a person lives in a constant state of nervous tension. Then, like timidity, the fear can become part of one's personality.

Timidity

Timidity can be defined as a propensity to show fear easily. It is associated with shyness, lack of confidence and an inability to be assertive. And there is usually an underlying, unrealistic fear of being thought silly or foolish, or seen to be inadequate or unattractive. Timid people tend to be oversensitive, apprehensive in new situations and very self-conscious, which is the feeling of being observed but not approved. Timidity, then, is linked with low self-esteem and, not being based on reality, is a form of free-floating anxiety. But in this case the anxiety, rather than being a generalised fear of threatening or dangerous people or events, revolves around others' perceptions of oneself.

Like anxiety states, no one is immune from this crippling form of fear. It can affect anyone, men or women, of all nationalities, cultures, and religious persuasions. It usually begins in childhood or early teens, the young person being withdrawn, unable to form close relationships, and prone to daydreaming. If untreated, it can persist into adult life when it is marked by a general immaturity, the adult still feeling like a submissive child overawed by powerful adults. Extreme timidity and shyness may eventually lead to a phobic state, in particular social phobia, which is an excessive fear of being in social situations.

Phobias

The word, "phobia", is Greek, and simply means "fear". But it has come to denote an irrational fear of specific objects, like dogs or spiders, or a situation, such as crossing over a bridge, driving a car, or making a speech. The fear is irrational, either because there is no actual danger, or because the fear is disproportional to the cause. A phobia of any kind may develop suddenly or build up slowly over many years; it can be a minor complaint or a crippling disorder. But even in the most severe cases, the intensity of the fear varies, being made worse by stress, tiredness or illness. Usually the fear is aroused only in the presence of the feared object, but a phobia may become obsessive. Then, thoughts of the feared object and the imagined effects of contact with it dominate a person's mind. Obsessive phobias often lead to compulsive behaviour. For instance, an obsessive fear of being made ill through exposure to germs may produce a compulsive urge to repeatedly wash one's hands.

There are many different kinds of phobias, the fear of germs being one of the more prevalent. But the most common is agoraphobia: the fear of open spaces. (The word, "agora", is Greek for "assembly" or "marketplace".) About two-thirds of agoraphobics are women, and the first onset usually occurs between the ages of eighteen and thirty-five. Phobias generally affect women more than men, and young people more than the elderly, with the exception of social phobias. This cluster, which includes fear of being in crowded places, fear of using the phone,

or of eating in company, is found equally in both sexes. Like all abnormal fears, phobias have always been in existence, although the incidence seems to be on the increase. For example, two thousand years ago Hippocrates described a man with an abnormal fear of flutes; and, less unusually, another with an abnormal fear of heights. Other common phobias include claustrophobia, which is a fear of enclosed spaces; and arachnophobia, which is an excessive fear of spiders. But just about anything can trigger a phobic response. And, when suddenly confronted with the feared object, the reaction may be one of panic.

Panic

Panic is a sudden upsurge of extreme terror, which can last anything from a few seconds to an hour or more. It is manifested in an uncontrollable urge to run, often with no clear plan in mind. Panic is often triggered, or exacerbated, by the reaction of others in dangerous situations, such as natural disasters or major accident, and the overwhelming fear makes it impossible to act calmly and rationally. In contrast, what are termed "panic attacks" do not have any obvious cause, and it is primarily these that constitute the fourth group of abnormal fears. Panic, or anxiety, attacks typically come on suddenly, and they quickly reach a peak of such intensity that breathing becomes difficult and the sufferer may think he is going to die. Then, gradually, the feelings of terror subside leaving him feeling weak and shaken. The attacks vary in frequency, from several times a day to once every few months or so. Between attacks there is often a vague sense of anxiety and there may be mild depression.

Panic attacks are often associated with agoraphobia, so are experienced more frequently by women than men. Like other forms of fear they usually begin in early adulthood, although they can occur for the first time at any age. Panic attacks, like phobias, are not as common as general anxiety states, but fear of the attacks themselves, and the shame of admitting to having them, can have an insidious, crippling effect, feeding and exacerbating the vague feeling of anxiety that accompanies them. Since there is an understandable fear of experiencing the attacks in public, they

16

increase any existing proneness to timidity and make agoraphobia and social phobias worse. The four classes of fear, then, result from and lead to the other types. So it is not surprising that many of the signs and symptoms also overlap.

In order to manage and eventually overcome fear, it is necessary first to understand it, which means not only differentiating between normal and abnormal fear and identifying your own specific forms of fear, but also learning to recognise the signs and symptoms. Signs are outward manifestations, visible to others, of an emotional or physical condition; symptoms are what you feel and experience inside. It is especially helpful if you can start becoming aware of fear in its early stages. The more sensitive you are to your own changing thoughts and feelings, and the more in tune with your own body, the quicker you will be able to deal with fear, before it starts to take hold.

SIGNS AND SYMPTOMS OF FEAR

Emotional Signs and Symptoms

People experience fear in different ways, and the same person may have a variety of symptoms at different times, which may or may not be outwardly visible. With free-floating anxiety and timidity there is a general sense of uneasiness, which is often accompanied by deep feelings of insecurity and vague fantasies revolving around possible mistakes, rejection, punishment and unforeseen circumstances that may lead to disaster. These imaginings, from which there is often no relief, tend to keep the sufferer continually upset and discouraged. In addition, there may be constant feelings of tiredness, irritability and tearfulness, due in part to disturbed sleep with dreams of being shot, choked, falling or being chased. In severe cases a person can feel strange or unreal, as if detached from the world around. All these signs and symptoms occur also with depression, and sometimes an underlying anxiety is missed because of the more easily recognised melancholy.

Those who have phobias or panic attacks experience similar effects, and again, these may be mistaken for, or actually

17

lead to, depression. However, when confronted by the feared object, or during a panic attack, these people also have a terrifying feeling that they are about to faint or die, scream out loud, lose control or go mad. Or they may have a strong urge to run or hide, or a sensation of being rooted to the spot. The emotional signs and symptoms, then, are linked with the physical: those felt in the body.

Physical Signs and Symptoms

Some of the physical manifestations of fear may be internal, so experienced only by the sufferer, or felt externally but without being too noticeable; others will be clearly visible to any observer. The most common signs and symptoms are a pounding or fluttering heart, dizziness and feelings of weakness, a sinking feeling in the stomach, muscle tension, sweating, tingling of the hands and feet, and dryness and tightness of the throat. These are typical for all types of fear, especially anxiety, but with timidity the fear may also show itself in blushing, facial tics, continual blinking or winking, trembling lips, tremor or jerky movements of the hands, and obvious breathlessness, the voice sometimes sounding high and squeaky. With phobias and panic attacks, the classic signs and symptoms also include headaches and back pains, muscle rigidity, pallor – with beads of sweat standing out on the face – staring eyes, and laboured breathing and gulping. With panic attacks there is likely also to be chest pain, a choking sensation, nausea, stomach cramps and an urgent need to urinate.

The physical signs and symptoms of fear occur because threat or danger triggers the stress reaction that prepares the body for fight or flight. This is a complex network of biochemical responses that is initiated by the sympathetic nervous system: part of the autonomic system that controls the heart and involuntary muscles. To begin with there is, among other things, a surge of adrenalin which causes the heart to beat faster and certain blood vessels to constrict, diverting oxygen away from the extremities and internal organs where it is not needed, towards the brain and major muscle groups. This explains the symptoms like palpitations, dizziness, pins and needles, upset stomach, etc.

It also explains why unchecked fear and stress damage the body, leading to such things as stroke or ulcers. (For a more detailed explanation of the stress reaction, see the book in this series, *Beyond Stress: Growing into serenity*.) Chronic fear also results in behavioural changes.

Behavioural Signs and Symptoms

Since fear triggers the stress reaction, it is not surprising that many of the behavioural signs and symptoms of chronic fear are identical with those that occur with stress — as well as depression. For instance, a classic sign of all three is sleep disturbance: an inability to get to sleep, restless sleep with bad dreams, or a tendency to wake in the night or too early in the morning. Other typical indications include a tendency to overeat or lack of appetite, a disinterest in sex, or difficulty summing up any enthusiasm for work or social pursuits, There may also be a general slowing down and an inability to complete tasks. When fear takes the form of phobia, the behavioural changes usually occur only when confronted with the feared object, and they are similar to those manifested during panic attacks. The phobic or panicked person may actually run away, scream, shout or lash out at someone; or he may freeze, standing rooted to the spot. In extreme cases, such as in combat situations, he may also lose control of bladder or bowel.

When there has been a major crisis, some people have a delayed reaction to fear. So, for instance, after a train crash or natural disaster, they may wander around looking dazed, or else stand motionless, unable to respond to simple questions. They might cling passively to people in authority and follow anyone's leadership automatically, or become irritable and aggressive. And long after the danger has passed there may be the onset of depression and apathy. These behaviours are associated with shock, and the body's reverting to its normal state after a very powerful fight or flight reaction.

Some behaviours resulting from fear are actually conscious or unconscious attempts to overcome the fear. These can be divided into three main groups, the first of which is counter-phobic behaviour. This occurs with phobias and is a compulsive

19

tendency to seek out the feared object in order to gain the mastery. For example, someone with a fear of heights may repeatedly stand on high bridges or look down from the top floor of tall buildings. The second group comprises various forms of obsessive-compulsive behaviour, which again are carried out with the aim of averting danger. Examples include constant checking or counting to avoid feelings of helplessness, or compulsive gambling, which is a drive to escape the pain of failure and loss. The third group consists of superstitious behaviour: the use of talismans, lucky mascots and the like, or carrying out ritualistic acts, with the purpose of warding off danger. Although these three classes of behaviours are attempts to deal with fear, they are unhealthy because they are triggered and perpetuated by the fears themselves. They are not calm, rational methods of overcoming fear.

You may not have realised that any difficulties you have coping with life can indicate an underlying fear, as well as stress or depression; or that a constant need to protect yourself means that you feel threatened and in danger. But the more you can accept that you are afraid, the more effectively you will be able to deal with your fear, and ultimately grow beyond it. While you increase your awareness of fear, you will need to practice taking note of the specific things that frighten you, whether in your personal life or the world at large, and observing your own emotional, physical and behavioural responses to threat or danger, until this becomes automatic. At the same time, it will help if you can start recognising, and understand, the more irrational causes of fear.

2

CAUSES AND EFFECTS OF
ABNORMAL FEAR

LEARNED MESSAGES OF FEAR

Fear Learned through Word

Like normal fear, excessive or irrational fear can be learned from others. During childhood, it can be learned in two primary ways, one of which is through how adults, especially parents, talk about threatening people or fearful situations. For instance, because so much press space is given to paedophile activities, parents may repeatedly warn their children not to speak to strangers or allow another adult to touch them, however innocent and caring the touch may be. Consequently, they give the impression that everyone is a potential abuser. A parent may also pass on his own insecurity by telling a child that it isn't safe to play outside or go to certain places; take up a sport, such as horse riding, for fear of accident; or attempt new skills for fear of failure. Frequent comments like, "Be careful...don't do that, you'll fall," will inevitably make a child afraid, causing him to anxiously hold back while others confidently go ahead.

A parent can also make a child afraid by threatening him with punishment – from themselves, bogeymen or God. Saying, for example, "If you're naughty I'll be ill and you'll have to go away," will make a child think that any misbehaviour will lead to dire consequences, so he will live in dread of making a wrong move. Similarly, threats, like, "If you don't do what you're told, the bogeyman will come and get you," are guaranteed to create an unnatural fear of punishment or retribution. When a child is told that God will punish him for any misdemeanour, he will also develop an unhealthy fear of God, who will be seen as harsh and punitive. He will therefore find it difficult in later life to form a close and satisfying relationship with God. In all these cases, the fear is exacerbated when children also witness their parents acting afraid.

Fear Learned through Deed

Actions always speak louder than words, so a child is more likely to learn fear through seeing a parent's fearful reactions than through what the parent says. And the fear is more likely to persist. Parents can show fear in many different ways, like acting nervously in the presence of authority figures, such as teachers or doctors; being too scared to stand up for themselves when confronted with angry or demanding relatives; being unable to assert their rights with shopkeepers; or being too frightened to go outside the home or attempt new skills. The child, then, learns through example to be anxious and timid. He may even acquire a phobia through this kind of modelling. A mother who, for example, hides in the cupboard whenever there is a thunderstorm, or who screams if she sees a spider, can instil this fear in her offspring, however much she tries to reassure him.

Children also learn to be afraid when a parent is over-protective. If a mother constantly fusses, anxiously saying things like, "You'll catch cold if you go out without your coat," or "You'll be ill if you don't go to sleep," the child will imbibe those fears and become overprotective of himself. It is especially harmful if a parent takes a child to the doctor at the slightest sniffle, or goes running to the school with every triviality. It is likely then that the child also will become a chronic worrier. And in addition to these direct results of parental fears, more subtle psychological dynamics are set in motion. When parents are afraid, they are unable to contain their children's fears, so the children experience them as overwhelming. As a result, they learn to be afraid of fear itself, and will eventually avoid anything that is even remotely threatening.

If, at any time in your life, you think you have been taught to be excessively or irrationally afraid, it will help if you can start recognising how this may have happened. This is not with the purpose of allocating blame, but in order to gain more understanding of your fears and start putting them in perspective. At the same time, you also need to identify those occasions when you may have been abnormally exposed to fear.

PERSONAL EXPERIENCE OF FEAR

Exposure to Physical Danger

Although fear is a normal response to threat or danger, sometimes it can be too intense or last longer than expected because the experience that triggered it was more traumatic than was realised. For instance, being abused, raped, or mugged, or being the victim of any violent or intrusive crime, can trigger such intense fear that the long-term psychological effects are devastating. Similarly, being involved in a traffic accident, such as a train or car crash, can give rise to a debilitating fear that, without help, may persist long after the event. Other examples include the fear aroused through being caught up in an environmental disaster, like a flood or earthquake. In all these cases, the abnormal fear, which is manifested in flashbacks and other incapacitating emotional and physical disturbances, is a major component of post-traumatic stress disorder.

23

An abnormal fear can also develop as a result of chronic exposure to threat or actual danger. The most pervasive and destructive is that experienced in childhood as a result of ongoing physical or sexual abuse, especially if the abuser was a parent or other carer. And witnessing abuse can be as harmful as experiencing it oneself. The fear is increased by feelings of isolation and helplessness that inevitably arise when there is no one to turn to for help, or if disclosure itself constitutes a danger. Likewise in later life, such things as domestic violence, threats and harassment from neighbourhood gangs, or racist attacks can lead to such deep terror that life becomes a constant, exhausting battle to survive. Living with fear is emotionally damaging, and when the physical threat or danger comes from people, it is especially so.

Exposure to Emotional Danger

Although any kind of danger has an emotional effect, it is classed as emotional when it directly hurts the soul: the thinking, feeling part of the self. The harm may be caused by such things as rejection, abandonment, disapproval, ridicule, constant criticism, or being intimidated or manipulated. These are all forms of emotional abuse, and the abuser can be anyone: a spouse or partner, friend, teacher, supervisor, religious leader.... The more the abuser was trusted and esteemed, and the greater the duration of the mistreatment, the more extensive is the damage and the longer it takes to repair. It is especially damaging if the abuse was experienced during the developmental years.

When emotional abuse occurs in childhood it is often unintentional, being due to a parent's ignorance or struggles with personal difficulties. But whether or not the harm was meant, the results are the same; and these include an enduring propensity to fear. Examples of emotional impairment in the formative years also include rejection for being disabled or the wrong sex; having a mother who was emotionally unavailable because she was harassed or depressed; losing a parent through death, separation or divorce; or being sent away unwillingly to a foster home or boarding school. However, the abuse may not have come from family members, but from peers, in the form of bullying or teasing, or being excluded from gangs or friendship groups. The sense of inferiority that these cruelties evoke is most likely to persist in the form of chronic anxiety or timidity.

In addition to those attitudes and behaviours that directly impair one's sense of emotional well-being, there is an added psychological danger that comes from being physically or sexually abused. Abuse of any kind creates fear, anger, guilt, and feelings of worthlessness and powerlessness. And it gives a subliminal message: your thoughts and feelings don't count, you are just there to be used. This undermining of self-esteem is a major factor in anxiety states and timidity; and the natural fear of the abuser makes one more susceptible to threat or danger than the average person, increasing the likelihood of phobia or panic attacks. Moreover, the normal fear that comes from being abused is likely to become generalised, creating a general inability to trust and a fear of emotional closeness.

When unhealthy fear develops in childhood, whether through exposure to abusive people or frightening situations or learned from parental figures, the emotional harm goes very deep. And, just as trampling on a seedling will cause more damage than stomping on a fully-grown tree, abnormal fear created in a young child will be more debilitating than that induced in an older one. This deep-rooted destruction of the soul makes it difficult, as adults, to deal with normal fears as and when they arise; and with every failure to cope, the damage is intensified.

25

If you suspect that a tendency to chronic or excessive fear began in childhood, then, in order to prevent further injury, you will have to go back to the roots. Only then can you grow beyond fear into faith. You can begin the process as you read the next section by noting also the less apparent ways in which your soul might have become impaired, and how the damage might have become obscured.

DEEP-ROOTED CAUSES OF FEAR

Unrecognised Trauma

When the mind is unable to cope with a frightening state of affairs, there is a tendency to push it away and think about something else; the memory is consciously suppressed. To some extent this is necessary in order to survive adverse circumstances and get on with life. But if this happens too frequently, the act of suppressing becomes an unconscious habit. The memories are then repressed, and there is no awareness of anything having been blocked out. An isolated happening that puts too much strain on the emotions may also be repressed, but this does not necessarily mean that one has been a victim of gross abuse, such as incest, witnessed a horrific death, or been involved in an appalling accident. Repression is a coping mechanism that allows a child – or adult – to cope with something that, at the time, is unbearable, but which could be handled at a later stage of development. However, because repression is an unconscious act, this particular defence tends to remain long after the trauma has passed, and beyond the point where it has become possible for the mind to face and accept it.

When a fearful memory has been repressed, the fear itself will remain but is likely to be experienced as a nameless dread or a vague sense of impending doom. Or it might be felt as constant agitation or unease that becomes more noticeable in certain situations or places. On the other hand, the fear can become so much a part of one's general make-up that it is no longer recognised at all, but instead experienced psychosomatically, as a physical disorder, or as cognitive interference: forgetfulness, inability to concentrate, difficulty learning.... Sometimes a person can feel stupid, not just because he has been told that he is, but because he has, in fact, shut down part of his own brain in order to repress an unthinkable thought.

When fear remains in its original form, it is sometimes displaced onto something less threatening. This is occasionally the case with phobias. For example, a child's father goes bankrupt and the family has to move to a smaller house. The child senses fear in the parents, knows that something dreadful has happened but, because it isn't talked about, is unable to deal with it. The new house is overrun with spiders and the child displaces his unexplained terror onto the spiders, and a phobia develops. Of course, a fear of spiders may simply be a fear of spiders, but when a phobia of any kind is not easily resolved, an underlying cause, such as unrecognised trauma, must be considered.

Wrongly Labelled Feelings

As well as being pushed down or displaced, a fear may also be disguised, taking on the form of another, more acceptable feeling. When this happens, the build-up of unmarked fear becomes itself a source of abnormality, making it difficult to cope with even minor threats or danger. Fear can assume just about any emotional shape, but most frequently it is disguised as anger, as these two emotions tend to go together. If you are a parent, you can probably recall an incident in which you shouted in anger at your child for doing something dangerous, like running across the road without looking, when what you were actually feeling was fear. At times fear can be swallowed up in anger, and this tends to happen when it is connected with an abusive or intimidating person. This is because it is easier to acknowledge being angry with someone than to admit to being afraid.

For the same reason, fear is sometimes wrongly labelled as courage. But stoical behaviour in painful or testing circumstances, rash acts of bravery, or a tendency to put oneself in dangerous situations could be a cover-up for fear. Fear can make a person feel weak, helpless and vulnerable, whereas courage, like anger, makes him feel strong and in control, although in this case the strength is an illusion.

Fear may also be disguised as sadness and dejection, which are the classic primary symptoms of depression, again because this is often easier to accept – and because it is easier to get help for this more familiar emotional disorder. The causes of depression are many, but two underlying factors are blocked memories and repressed anger, both of which for various reasons have been too frightening to face. Fear, then, is concealed at the very heart of depression. The same applies with stress, which is the biochemical fight or flight response that is activated by fear.

Surprisingly, fear can also be disguised as love. The Bible teaches that perfect love casts out fear: the two are opposites. And when fear arises because of feeling trapped with someone who is abusive or violent, it is easier to kid oneself, consciously or otherwise, that the reverse is true and that the captivating element is love. When love is a cover-up for fear it can be recognised by its painful intensity and exclusivity: the "loved" person takes over, slowly and insidiously, until he becomes one's entire world. By this time, the feeling of ardour can be so overpowering that it is difficult to see what is really there underneath. But with this and any other disguise, the underlying fear has to be faced and dealt with, otherwise it will infiltrate every area of life, eroding an already damaged self-esteem.

Damaged Self-esteem

Fear and low self-esteem are connected, because some of the causes and many of the effects are the same. One's sense of self can be damaged in many ways, one of which is through exposure to a threatening person or terrifying situation. Any traumatic event inevitably creates, not only an upsurge of fear, but also a residual feeling of vulnerability and helplessness; a disturbing awareness of no longer being in control of one's own destiny. This disruption of the natural drive towards autonomy and self-fulfilment produces, in turn, an underlying insecurity: an urge to keep looking over one's shoulder, expecting at any time to be overwhelmed by unexpected adverse circumstances. Fear, in this case, is a result of one's own imagination and a classic symptom of free-floating anxiety. It may also have some bearing on the propensity to panic attacks.

When there has been mistreatment of any kind – emotional, physical or sexual – it also creates feelings of worthlessness and insignificance. This naturally erodes one's conception of self as a valuable individual with unique strengths and abilities and great creative potential. And the failure to recognise and accept one's essential worth leads to a withdrawal from social situations and an avoidance of any opportunity to stretch oneself and fulfil one's dreams and ambitions. The more one withdraws, the more difficult it becomes to voice one's own views and opinions, be assertive, make decisions and deal with confrontation. And the associated fear of rejection makes it hard to express feelings or form close relationships. This inability to value oneself, along with feelings of vulnerability and helplessness, is also at the root of many anxiety states, and is a primary cause of timidity.

Especially injurious to self-esteem is emotional abuse, the more so if it occurred during the formative years when one's sense of self is still being developed. Children believe what their parents tell them, and if they are repeatedly told that they are stupid, ugly, no good, or will never amount to anything, they will eventually come to believe it. They will also be harmed by such things as unrealistic parental expectations and constant rejection of their accomplishments as substandard. In later life their self-esteem will be further impaired by their tendency to either give up or drive themselves, in an attempt to prove their parents wrong, especially as their inevitable feeling of inferiority will get in the way, preventing success. Their repeated failures will damage self-esteem even more, and create yet more fear, manifested chiefly as social phobia: fear of meeting fresh people, going to novel places, and trying out new skills.

Low self-esteem, then, like fear, comes from being harmed, physically or emotionally, and the damage causes one's perceptions to become distorted, so there is a false view of oneself, others and God. If your self-esteem is low you may, for instance, see yourself as unlovable, ugly or stupid; you may experience others as superior, critical or unfriendly; and perceive God to be harsh, punitive, uncaring, or even absent. Therefore, in order to improve self-esteem, and at the same time grow beyond fear, you first have to accept that you may not be seeing things as they really are. You will also need to open your mind to the possibility of unrecognised trauma and the existence of fear in disguise. As your internal vision begins to clear, you will then find yourself losing the need to keep fighting, running or hiding.

THE EFFECTS OF UNHEALTHY FEAR

Unprovoked Attack

When there is a deep-rooted sense of unrelieved fear, there is a compulsive urge to either fight or flee. This is because everyone, including one's own self, is perceived as a potential enemy. The tendency to fight oneself can be physical; self-harm may be prompted by unrecognised fear as well as anger. But often the attacks are more subtle and the self is injured through such things as smoking, drug-taking or excessive drinking. Fear can also result in a susceptibility to illness or accident proneness. But more usually the attacks are verbal and take the form of constantly putting oneself down, thereby destroying one's own confidence.

When fear triggers an urge to attack others, the assaults are again usually verbal, although there may also be a desire to inflict physical harm. For instance, a dread of being thought stupid can make someone speak scathingly of others' comments, and a fear of being thought unattractive can make him hypercritical of others' appearance. Verbal attacks may also take the form of interrupting, dismissing others' thoughts and opinions, or monopolising the conversation. Or they can be more insidious, manifested perhaps through backhanded compliments or sarcasm. Aggression can also be shown through body language: scowling face, clenched hands, rigid posture, or actively turning away. With all of these, the underlying cause is a propensity to reject or harm others before they reject or harm you.

Along with the fear of rejection from others is the fear that God will turn away, or perhaps mete out some dire punishment for minor shortcomings. As with other people, this can lead to a compulsion to repudiate God first. Rejection is a form of attack, as are angry accusations, such as "God isn't there!", "He never listens!", "He doesn't care!". With God too, it can feel safer to express anger, contempt or unbelief than to admit to being needy and afraid of being abandoned. Unlike verbal assaults, attacks on God cannot be directly physical, so these are often displaced onto religious institutions or people. And when the fear is on a national scale, the result can be war in God's name.

Excessive Avoidance

Internal conflict, embattled relationships with others and enmity with God are all highly stressful, so it is often easier to deal with fear through avoidance. Self-avoidance is an inability to accept and acknowledge parts of the self, and this makes it impossible to deal with and change the negative traits, or make use of and enjoy the positive. The more one avoids looking inside oneself, the more one fears to look, because of what might be discovered. The common expression, "He is afraid of his own shadow", is an indication of this dread of seeing what is lurking in the deep recesses of the soul. When the fear isn't faced, all sorts of horrific things are imagined.

An unhealthy avoidance of others also comes from a fear of imagined dangers. For instance, someone who is afraid of ridicule or humiliation might refrain from saying anything at all, in case his words bring about this hurtful response. A person who is afraid of being thought fat might avoid going swimming or jogging, and so find it difficult to lose weight; and someone who is afraid of failure will avoid any tasks or situations, such as college courses, where failure is a possibility. The fear of rejection is especially powerful, and this can lead to a reluctance to make friends, an avoidance of closeness and intimacy, and an unwillingness to risk commitment of any kind, especially marriage. The fear might be so intense that all company is shunned. Avoidance might seem the easy way, but it keeps a person bound and impoverished, in all areas of life.

In the spiritual arena, an unhealthy fear of God will lead to a propensity to hide from God. This may take the form of denying God's existence, so kidding oneself that there is no one out there to see or care. Or, it may take the form of excessive piety: always smiling, praising God, expressing only positive thoughts and feelings instead of telling it like it is. The compulsion to hide from God is linked with the fear of rejection and punishment, and has been in existence since the beginning of time. When Adam, the first man, sinned, the first thing he did was hide from God's presence. And when God asked him why he hiding, he replied, "I was afraid." Fear is the opposite of faith, as well as love, and keeps us from coming to God openly and confidently. It cuts us off from God, as well as ourselves and other people, and leads also to a fearful urge to build protective walls around ourselves, when no protection is needed.

Unnecessary Protection

Protection from fear can take the form of building psychological defences. One of these is denial. For instance, if a child is being abused, he may deny to himself that it is happening. Or he may escape the reality of abuse through excessive daydreaming, imagining himself in another place, in another time, with different parents or circumstances. A similar defence is shutdown. Thoughts and feeling, even physical ones, can be switched off, so that pain and all the associated emotions, including fear, are not felt. Withdrawal – as discussed – is also a form of defence, as is the drive to perfectionism. This protects the self from the knowledge of one's own limited strengths and abilities, and of one's own immortality.

The excessive need to shelter from imagined facets of the self or external dangers is also shown in ritualistic behaviour. For instance, in order to protect himself from a known or unknown fear, someone might make a point of always getting dressed in the same order or always going the same way to work – and feeling anxious if he has to deviate. Or he may devise a set of words or phrases that he has to say at specific times. Even prayer, which should be a spontaneous opening up to God, can become ritualistic: a way of containing fear. In extreme form, this protective urge is manifested in obsessive-compulsive behaviour. The need to keep repeating actions unnecessarily, like hand-washing or checking doors and windows, is an attempt to keep fear at bay.

Another way of protecting oneself, when there is often no need for protection, is through the use of such things as amulets, lucky charms, talismans, St Christopher's medals and the like. Even a crucifix can be used in this way. If it is worn, not as an expression of faith, but because of a belief in its efficacy to guard against danger, then it is an indication of fear and insecurity. When a child is afraid, he holds on more tightly to his comfort blanket. In adulthood, these take many different forms, and the greater the fear the more imperative is the need to have and retain them. "Comfort blankets" can only be relinquished as the fear is recognised and faced, and dealt with in more constructive ways.

If you are constantly afraid, then as well as identifying the type of fear and its possible causes and effects, it is also helpful if you can recognise your own particular ways of dealing with fear. Maybe you tend to go on the attack, or perhaps you avoid people and situations that you perceive to be frightening, or turn to artificial means of protection. But of greatest importance is that you admit to yourself that you are afraid and acknowledge the full extent of your fear. You may have hidden this awareness from yourself, telling yourself perhaps that you were born with a timid disposition and that's just the way you are, or that you can't help your panic attacks; they are a recognised medical disorder.

It is human and normal to be afraid. It is not necessarily a sign of weakness or cowardice. The greatest achievers and most renowned warriors in history have experienced fear, as have the most spiritual of people. The Bible is full of such examples; men and women who were afraid, often with good reason, at other times without. Some of these were overcome and destroyed by their anxieties and insecurities, others learned to cope with their feelings. And many were able to grow beyond fear into a solid and enduring faith in themselves, others and God. We will look now at some of these examples.

3

EXAMPLES AND INSPIRATION

HOW OTHERS CAN HELP

Giving Reassurance

People often don't like admitting that they are afraid, even to themselves. They might say that they are anxious or worried; they may even confess to having panic attacks, on the basis that this is something they can't help. But they will not accept that they are afraid, even when they know that anxiety, worry and panic are simply different manifestations of fear. It helps, therefore, to know that other people experience fear, especially when those others are brave men, renowned for their courage in battle, or women who have gone down in history as heroines, having courageously faced physical or emotional danger. It reassures us that we are not weak, or have a yellow streak, but that we are, in fact, experiencing a normal human emotion.

As well as feeling weak, people also tend to feel guilty for being afraid. This is often a hangover from childhood days as many parents fail to recognise or understand a child's terror, dismissing it with comments like, "Don't cry. Be a brave boy!" or, "Stop making a fuss. There's nothing to be afraid of." In Christian circles especially, guilt may be induced because of the mistaken belief that even normal fear is an indication of lack of faith. This, rather than helping, creates yet more anxiety. We start to feel that there must be something terribly wrong with us: that we must be emotionally or spiritually immature, or even dysfunctional. At these times, it reassures us to read of great warriors like the Psalmist David, who wrote openly and honestly about his battles with fear.

David was often afraid – and with good reason. At one stage he was concerned about his marital difficulties, worried about the way his children were going, and afraid of his envious and vindictive father-in-law, King Saul. As an exile he often didn't know where his next meal was coming from, or how he would provide for his men. And he was anxious about the political situation as self-seeking men obtained positions of power then went back on their promises, twisting their words so that no one knew where they stood. David was afraid for himself, his family and his nation, and his fears are ones we can identify with today. This reassures us, not only that we are not weak, cowardly or spiritually inadequate, but also that bad times pass. And, it gives us courage.

Offering Encouragement

When we hear or read about others who have bravely faced cruel tyrants or adverse circumstances, it stirs something in our own psyche, enabling us to get in touch with our own inner strength and courage. Fear can be so overwhelming that we lose touch with the stronger parts of ourselves and forget the many times when we too have bravely dealt with pain, loss or danger. Instead, we tell ourselves that we will always be a prey to fear, and that there is nothing we can do to change a situation, whether in our own family or workplace, or in our country as a whole. When we have reached this stage, someone like David, or the Old Testament hero, Gideon, can embolden us to face our fears and deal with any threat or peril.

Gideon lived at a time when the Israelites were under constant attack from the Midianites, and they were reduced to threshing their wheat in secret, to avoid being plundered. At first, Gideon was reluctant to take on the task of leadership and rebel against their oppressors. He was a humble man and saw himself as the least important man in the least important tribe. But with repeated encouragement from God he was able to rouse a handful of his people to attack the Midianites, and conquer them. Encouragement, like fear, is catching. It inspires us to push ourselves on, to achieve greater and better things.

Providing Inspiration

It is human nature to look to others for inspiration. This is why we create superheroes and heroines whom we can admire and emulate. In our most fearful moments we imagine being like them, or even being them. But while this is helpful up to a point, enabling us to get in touch with our own higher ideals, it does not empower us to deal realistically with fear. It is primarily for this reason that biblical heroes and heroines are presented with all their flaws and weaknesses. They were not superheroes with perfect faith who achieved impossible goals. On the contrary. They were normal human beings who got angry, upset, depressed, stressed out, and who were often afraid. Their inspiration comes from their honesty in revealing their innermost feelings and describing, not only their exploits and triumphs, but also the times when they flunked it – like, for instance, the prophet Jonah.

God had told Jonah to go to the city of Nineveh, to warn the people that, unless they repented, God would wipe them out. Jonah, not unnaturally, didn't want to go to Nineveh. The people there were his nation's enemy, and it would be much safer for everyone if God did wipe them out. So he ran away, boarding a ship that was heading in the opposite direction. But, after a series of catastrophes, he overcame his fear and associated depression and successfully carried out his commission. In Jonah's case his success came because he discovered that it was easier to face his fears than run from them. Sometimes it is sensible to flee from a dangerous situation, but it is never wise to turn one's back on fear.

Another man who found that fleeing from fear isn't a good idea was the prophet, Elijah. He had just experienced a tremendous victory at Carmel, having proved that his God was greater than the false god, Baal. But then, hearing that the wicked Queen Jezebel was going to kill him, he panicked and fled into the wilderness. Elijah was also experiencing a classic psychological letdown, such that he wanted to die, but he was helped by the basic physical provision of food and drink, and by the reassurance that he wasn't the only one resisting Queen Jezebel's command to worship Baal.

If you have ever been in a situation that challenged your convictions; or, like David, had family or financial worries or been anxious about today's failing morality, then perhaps you too have felt that you were alone, and even that the whole world was against you. If so, you will have discovered that this creates yet more fear, making you want to go on the attack or hide behind your defences. Perhaps also, like Gideon or Jonah, you have felt weak and insignificant, and totally unsuited to the task, and your fear has made you want to run. But, however fear has affected you, it helps to be reminded, not only to look after your basic physical needs, which tend to get neglected when fear is all-pervasive, but to stop running and start looking around you. The world is full of people with high ideals, who stand for truth and right; people you can trust to stand by you in times of trouble, providing reassurance, encouragement and inspiration.

Having high ideals and living up to them is important because when, through fear, you damage your own sense of integrity, you actually do become estranged, not only from other people and God, but also from yourself. This is what happened to King Saul, a man who had so much potential but failed to fulfil it because fear got in the way. We will look in some detail at his story, then at the history of the Jewish Queen, Esther, who overcame her natural fear in order to save her people from a holocaust. We will conclude with Timothy the timid who, with the support of his mentor, the apostle Paul, was enabled to grow beyond fear to become a respected Christian leader.

A KING'S INSECURITY

Saul's Potential

Saul, the son of Kish of the tribe of Benjamin, was the first king of Israel. He came from a powerful, wealthy family and was himself impressive, described as being without equal. He stood head and shoulders above other men, and his courage matched his physique. Israel was, at this time, under pressure from warring Philistines, and the people thought that only a king could bring them deliverance. The prophet, Samuel, warned them what would happen if they had a king like the nations around them: young men would be drafted into the army or forced to work in the king's fields and vineyards, young women would be taken to serve in the palace, and crippling taxes demanded of everyone.

But the people refused to listen. So, guided by God, Samuel secretly anointed Saul as king.

Saul was amazed. He asked Samuel if he'd got the right man. After all, his tribe was the smallest, and his clan the most insignificant in that tribe. Whether this was modesty or lack of faith in himself is debatable. What we do know is that after his anointing Saul demonstrated a new spirituality and began acting with authority, ignoring the taunts of those who failed to recognise his new status. And when Israel was besieged by the Ammonites, Saul's courage, organising ability and personal integrity proved his right to rule. After this victory, Samuel confirmed Saul's position as king in a public ceremony. Saul was now thirty, and he ruled for forty-two years. But his reign was not a successful one. Saul started well, but his lack of self-knowledge and faith in himself and God, and his increasing anxiety set him on a downward path to destruction.

Saul's Fears

Saul was, at times, very understandably afraid of the Philistines with their massed chariots and highly trained foot soldiers. And it was during an assault by this persistent enemy that Saul's fear got the better of him. Many Israelites had fled and were hiding in caves and thickets, quaking with terror, while Saul waited anxiously for Samuel to come and make sacrifices to God and pray for deliverance. He waited the appointed seven days, but when Samuel failed to arrive and his troops began to scatter, Saul panicked and, taking upon himself the priestly role, offered the sacrifices himself. He had no sooner completed his offering when Samuel turned up, and Saul could give no real explanation for his blatant disobedience, except that he was afraid. Samuel told him that, because of his lack of trust, his kingdom would be taken from him and given to another: a man after God's own heart.

This was a double blow to Saul: to be deprived of his kingdom and lose God's favour! And this activated another fear: that of rejection. Yet he was at first very taken with his replacement, the young shepherd boy, David, who had come to his notice when he slew the nine-foot tall Philistine, Goliath. The death of their champion caused the Philistine armies to flee, with the Israelites in hot pursuit. But when, afterwards, the women danced and sang in the streets, "Saul has slain his thousands, and David his ten thousands," [1] Saul's fear of being replaced in the people's affections, as well as God's, turned to an insane jealousy.

As a result, Saul went back on his promise to David, giving him his youngest daughter, Michal, in marriage, instead of the eldest. But rather than alleviating his fear and jealousy, they were inflamed, because it turned out that Michal loved David. Then Saul realised that his own son, Jonathan, had also formed a close bond with this popular and successful young man. Saul's increasing terror led him to strip David of his military honours, physically attack him, and ultimately banish him. In later years, Saul's fear of rejection turned to paranoia: he became convinced that everyone was against him.

To some extent, Saul's fears were well founded. But his dread of rejection made him reject, with the result that many actually did turn against him. However, Saul's greatest renunciation came not from his children or people, but from God. And his being out of touch with God made him susceptible to his own increasingly black moods and moments of panic. At these times he tried desperately to win God's love and approval, through making rash vows and uncalled for sacrifices, supposedly to honour God – although the monument he had built was in honour of himself! And he repeatedly excused his actions, saying that he was afraid of the people so he'd gone along with what *they* wanted. But Samuel was not deceived. He accused Saul of arrogance and eventually severed all contact with him. Even then, Saul would not face his fear and deal with it, and after Samuel's death, when Saul could no longer get any response from God, his fear drove him to the witch of Endor. The unexpected outcome terrified the witch and Saul, and confirmed his estrangement from God and unfitness to rule.

Saul's Downfall

Saul's downfall came about because he was unable to deal with fear, which was at the root of many of his problems. It was fear that made him incapable of waiting when Samuel failed to arrive at the expected time to offer sacrifices. Saul's attitude was a peeved, "If Samuel isn't here to do it, then I'll just get on with it myself." His self-reliance was not, in this case, a sign of strength, but of lack of faith. Saul couldn't trust Samuel, or God, so he was unable to calmly stand still, knowing that it would be alright. He had to rush into doing something, to hold himself and his army together.

Saul's fear meant also that he was unable to connect. His rash vows and uncalled for sacrifices were unacceptable because they were being used as a means of control. He thought that by making promises to God, or giving gifts – that were not actually his to give – he could get God to do what he wanted. His gifts were not given humbly, as offerings of love; they were used as talismans, and his sacrifices as rituals, to invoke some kind of protection. But Saul learned to his cost that God could not be manipulated in this way. And the result, rather than the growth of an increasing faith in God's goodness and care, was a sense of estrangement that left him, more than ever, a prey to his own uncontrollable anger and jealousy.

Saul might have been spared if he could have learned from his mistakes. But again, fear got in the way. This would have meant, first of all, having the courage to admit that he had got it wrong. Saul was able to do this verbally, but it was just words. There was no ability to humbly reflect on his actions, and no true repentance. Instead, Saul committed the ultimate act of rebellion by going to a witch, thinking in his arrogance and total lack of understanding that this would reconnect him with God. After this, it was all downhill for Saul. He was severely wounded in battle with the Philistines, and his fear of being abused by his enemy made him commit suicide. Right to the end, he was unable to trust God to protect him, and he fell upon his own sword.

Saul's story is a tragic one. He had so much potential – hence his being chosen as king. But he had a fatal flaw: his deep insecurity and inability to trust. Perhaps you can identify with Saul's insecurity; it is something we all feel at times. But the question is, what are you doing with it? Do you focus exclusively on your physical strengths, successes and achievements in order to avoid looking at the insecure, frightened part of your self? Or do you perhaps, like Saul, feel that you have to rush into doing something, anything, to keep your fear in abeyance? Do you have a tendency to manipulate and control? If any of these apply, then you need to look honestly at the fear that prompts these pseudo-coping methods and learn to trust yourself, others and God. Then, rather than stifling your potential, you can enhance it and, like Queen Esther, start discovering strengths you didn't know you possessed.

A QUEEN'S ANXIETY

Esther's Danger

Esther, a Jewess, was the wife of the Persian King Ahasuerus, known in Greek as Xerxes, who ruled from 486 to 465 BC. His empire was vast, stretching from India to northern Ethiopia, and he was known for his debauchery and bloodshed. The Greek historian, Herodotus, described him as capricious, cruel and sensual. Esther's story merged with that of her sadistic and lascivious husband in 479 BC, through the offices of her cousin, Mordecai, who had brought her up after the deaths of her parents. Mordecai's ancestor, along with many other Jews, had been taken into captivity by Nebuchadnezzar, king of Babylon, and chosen to remain after the empire was conquered by the Persians.

The sequence of events that brought Esther to the king's notice had begun four years earlier when Ahasuerus, as was customary, asked his wife, Vashti, to join him at a great feast, the culmination of six months display of opulence and power. When Vashti refused to join him, he was enraged. And, on the advice of his astrologers, he disposed of her. He meant, perhaps, for this to be only a temporary measure, but Vashti had been involved in a power struggle with the nobles, who didn't want her reinstated. So, after four years of disastrous wars with the Greeks, when Ahasuerus began thinking again about his former queen, they suggested that he choose another wife, waiving the rule that he select one from among the nobility. Consequently, all the beautiful women in his winter capital of Susa were brought to the palace for a year's beauty treatment, prior to being presented to the king. And among them was Esther.

Jewish tradition places Esther among the three most beautiful women who ever lived. And it was perhaps her beauty that ensured she was the one chosen. We are not told how Esther felt about this, but given Ahasuerus's character, it is unlikely that she relished her new position. Then, she was confronted with another danger: Mordecai refused to pay the homage demanded by the king's favourite official, Haman. And Haman was so angry he resolved to wipe out all the Jews in Persia, who were now scattered throughout the 127 provinces. Being very superstitious, he chose a lucky day eleven months off, and gained the king's consent by accusing the Jews of treason and promising him vast sums of plundered money – which, following the Greek wars, Ahasuerus was badly in need of. When Mordecai got to hear of this, he asked Esther to intercede on the Jews' behalf, she being one of the few people with access to the king.

Esther's Courage

It is difficult to imagine the fear Esther must have felt on discovering that her entire race was going to be wiped out, or her terror at having to risk approaching the king. She told Mordecai that she couldn't do it, reminding him that the king had only one penalty for those who came uninvited into the inner court – death. To make matters worse, she was not currently in favour; she hadn't seen her husband for a month. But Mordecai insisted, saying that sooner or later the king would discover their kinship and know that she was Jewish, and the fact of her being queen would not protect her from the impending holocaust. So, with the famous resigned words, "If I perish, I perish," Esther agreed to face her husband, reveal her nationality and request his help. First, however, she asked Mordecai to organise a three day fast.

Bolstered by the prayers of her people – which, for the Jews, always went with fasting, but was presumably too dangerous to write about, along with any mention of God – Esther approached the king. To her vast relief he held out his sceptre and asked her what she wanted. She replied only that she would like to invite him and Haman to a banquet. Ahasuerus accepted the invitation for both of them, and at the end of the feasting he asked Esther again to make her petition. He would give her anything she desired, up to half of his kingdom. It would appear that Esther intended to make her request at this point, while her husband was in a compliant mood, but her courage failed her. So instead, she invited him and Haman to another banquet. In the meantime, Haman was so incensed by Mordecai's continuing lack of respect that he had a gallows built on which to hang him.

Then, during a sleepless night, while the king was being read the court records, Ahasuerus discovered that Mordecai hadn't been rewarded for revealing a plot, and he asked Haman how this could best be done. Haman, mistakenly thinking that he was the one to be honoured, suggested the highest public acclaim; and his subsequent disappointment and humiliation was still rankling when, having led Mordecai on a triumphal procession through the streets of the capital, he was forced to hurry with the king to the second banquet. After this feast, Queen Esther took her life into her hands, admitted she was Mordecai's cousin and therefore Jewish, and told the king what Haman had plotted.

Esther's Triumph

The king was so shocked that he temporarily left Esther alone, during which time Haman flung himself onto her couch, pleading for his life. When the king returned and found Haman in this compromising position he accused his favourite of trying to molest the queen, and Haman was hanged on the gallows he had earlier built for Mordecai. Then the king promoted Mordecai, giving him Haman's old position, the highest in the land after his own. According to Persian law, Ahasuerus could not revoke his edict regarding the slaughter of the Jews, so instead he issued a second one, giving the Jews the right to defend themselves, and a proclamation to this effect was rushed to all 127 provinces.

The Jews, now being in favour, found many to support them. And on the day Haman had selected for the holocaust they defeated their attackers, killing 500 men in the city of Susa alone, including Haman's ten sons, and a further 75,000 throughout the Persian Empire. Afterwards, Mordecai issued an edict, making this a day to be celebrated annually, which it is to this day: the Feast of Purim. The word comes from the Persian word, "pur", meaning "lot", because Haman cast lots to decide which would be his lucky day.

Esther's fear must, at times, have been overwhelming but, unlike Saul, she had a quiet faith in her cousin, as well as in God. She was able to wait, to reflect and calmly assess the situation, and ultimately rise above her fears – which are given scant mention. Her courage undoubtedly came in part from the realisation that there was nowhere to run; she had to face her fears or die. But mostly it came from her love and concern for her people. Esther was able to discover that, "There is no fear in love, but perfect love casts out fear." [2] And because of this she was able to prove God's faithfulness and power, and her own ability to influence events.

You will probably never have to face danger to the extent that Esther did. But perhaps you have to make a stand that will put your career in jeopardy or be the death of a long-cherished hope. Or maybe you feel trapped in your own little world and so consumed with fear that you are unable to feel concern for anyone else. You can learn from Esther, then, that truth and love are the keys to overcoming fear and developing faith, and that this applies whether your fears revolve around your own safety, a family situation, or the state of today's world. As you start looking outward, thinking about the welfare of others, as well as your own integrity, your fears will shrink and faith will grow. It is an upward spiral, and one that was also discovered by the young man, Timothy, as he accompanied the apostle Paul on his missionary journeys.

A LEADER'S TIMIDITY

Timothy's Struggles

Timothy, who possibly became a Christian when Paul visited his home town of Lystra — in present-day Turkey — during his first missionary journey, was the son of a mixed marriage: his mother was Jewish and his father Greek. So, from the beginning he never really belonged in one group or the other. This may have been the beginning of his struggles with timidity and self-doubt, and his propensity to physical ailments. But, in spite of this, he was able to gain the approbation of the elders in

45

his local church. And when Paul returned to Lystra some years later with his co-worker, Silas, he heard such good reports of the young man, and was so impressed with his potential, that he asked Timothy to accompany him and Silas on their second missionary tour.

With his church's blessing, Timothy joined the team, and he soon proved himself affectionate, loyal and capable. As a result, he was entrusted with increasingly more responsibility. When, for instance, Paul moved on from Thessalonica, he left Timothy and Silas there with a special commission to encourage the Christians who were being persecuted for their faith. Later, the two were given the important task of following up and consolidating Paul's work in Berea.

However, Timothy's timid disposition and lack of faith in himself meant that he was easily swayed by others. He was especially intimidated by older men, which at times made it difficult for him to assert his authority. And he tended to ignore positive comments about his performance, focusing instead on his youth and inexperience. In addition, Timothy was often unwell, having recurring stomach upsets. These were possibly psychosomatic: physical symptoms of his chronic insecurity.

Timothy's Support

Despite Timothy's diffidence and hesitancy, Paul stood by him, constantly helping and encouraging him. Early in their relationship he had become a father figure, often referring to Timothy as "my son in the faith". And it was through Paul's love and support that Timothy was able to acquire a firmer sense of his national and religious identity, and a more realistic, therefore healthier, self-concept.

Timothy's self-esteem was also boosted by Paul's constant reminders of the solid grounding in Jewish doctrine he'd been given by his mother and grandmother, his Christian calling, and the fact that his church had recognised his ministerial gifts. He was further helped by Paul's encouragement to recognise his strengths and know his own mind, to hold onto his values and beliefs and not be intimidated by his elders or swayed by the opinions or moral standards of others. He was even urged to look after himself physically, to make sure he had good nourishment and exercise. And he was given practical advice about the treatment of his recurring stomach disorder.

Timothy, moreover, had proof of Paul's faith in him through the letters of commendation sent to various church leaders. For instance, Paul wrote to the Corinthians saying that they should accept Timothy because he was carrying out God's work, just as he himself was, and they should ensure that he had nothing to fear during his stay with them. [3] Similarly, Paul highly recommended Timothy to the Philippians, saying that he had no one else like him, who took such a genuine interest in their welfare. [4] Timothy was, by now, able to stop focusing on his own inadequacies and take an interest in others because Paul had first taken an interest in him.

Timothy's Development

As Timothy continued to gain confidence in himself, learning to trust and value his own thoughts and opinions, he became increasingly more relaxed with others, and better able to win their esteem – not now as a young Christian, but as a leader, entirely responsible for the running of a local church. This in turn increased his faith in himself. But it had needed a father figure like Paul to start this upward spiral. Timothy's capacity to gain the respect and trust of this wise and venerable man must have gone a long way towards enabling him to respect and believe in himself. Paul's help and support also enabled Timothy to grow and develop spiritually, and possibly also improve his physical health. But perhaps Paul's greatest gift to Timothy was the enhancement of his own unique personality, which enabled him to become independent.

Much of Paul's urging towards self-trust and autonomy is recorded in his first letter to Timothy. In his second, written from prison where he had been incarcerated for his faith, Paul reminded his protégé that, since there was no hope of his release, Timothy would now have to stand on his own two feet. And Paul encouraged him yet again to trust his own abilities and judgments and not be dependent on the opinions of others. By this time a close bond had developed between the two, who knew each other well, and Paul spoke of his longing to see Timothy again, recalling his sincere faith, affection and loyalty. Over the years, Paul had been a great help to Timothy. But Timothy had also become a great help to Paul.

If, like Timothy, you have a tendency to be timid and retiring, you may, like him, have also discounted your positive attributes and therefore feel that you are no use to anyone. But everyone has strengths and abilities that can be nurtured and developed – although first you have to recognise and appreciate them. In order to do this, you ideally need an apostle Paul in your life: someone who can point them out to you and keep reminding you of them. This can be a spouse, friend, church leader, or anyone who has faith in your abilities and is concerned about your spiritual and psychological development. Or it can be a composite of several people who can build you up in different ways. But you have to listen to your supporters, and believe them. There is no point in their building you up if, at the same time, you keep putting yourself down.

If you have not yet found such a person, perhaps you can begin by applying to your own situation the relevant experiences of Saul, Esther or Timothy – or any other historical character who has been a warning or inspiration to you. As, with them, you start out on the journey from fear to faith, sooner or later you will find others waiting to assist you along the road. Meanwhile, it will help if you can also learn some coping skills, so that fear does not slow you down – or worse, make you turn aside.

4

COPING WITH FEAR

FACE THE REALITY OF FEAR

Identify your Fears

In order to develop some control over fear, it is first essential to accept and acknowledge its existence. This involves also facing up to the reality of any trauma that may have triggered the fear. Pretending that you are not afraid, or denying any past abuse or trauma, will make it impossible for you to move forward: you cannot outgrow something that has never been! Where there has been childhood abuse this will be particularly difficult, and you may need to consider professional help in the form of counselling or psychotherapy.

Having admitted to yourself that you are afraid, you then need to decide which type of fear you most struggle with – anxiety, timidity, phobia or panic – and identify the things that frighten you most. There are different ways of managing excessive or abnormal fears, depending on the form they take, and in order to find the most effective method you must be clear about what you are dealing with.

It is easier to manage fear before it becomes excessive or prolonged, so it will help if you can develop an awareness of your own signs and symptoms, becoming especially alert to the earliest warnings. Do you, for example, first become conscious of fear through emotional symptoms, such as apprehension or jitteriness, or a sense of unreality? Or do you first notice physical symptoms: your heart fluttering, stomach knotting, feelings of nausea, etc? Have you been taking notice of behavioural signs, like sleep disturbance or eating disorders? If you have not been in the habit of monitoring any dysfunctional ways of coping, or have attributed them to the wrong cause, your propensity to fear may be greater than you think.

Acknowledge the Severity of your Fear

In order to deal fully with fear, and in the best possible way, you must have an accurate assessment of its severity. For example, if your fear doesn't greatly affect your way of life, restricting you only in a few social situations, then enlisting the support of your family and implementing a few coping skills may be all that is required. You may even decide that you don't need to do anything at all. But if your fear is so bad that you cannot face people under any circumstances, or hold down a job, then reading this book and putting it into practice may be only the first step on a long journey to recovery. When fears are deep-rooted they are not eliminated overnight, so you need to be realistic about the time it will take to grow beyond fear, and be patient with yourself.

Admitting the severity of your fear means acknowledging also the effect it has on those closest to you. For instance, if you are a chronic worrier, this can have a depressing effect on the people you live with; whilst being excessively timid makes it hard for friends and acquaintances. It is difficult keeping up a conversation with someone who answers only in monosyllables. If you have a phobia, or a tendency to panic, that severely restricts your own life, it will also limit, to some extent, the lives of your immediate family. And it can place a heavy burden on them, requiring, perhaps, that they do your shopping, ferry the children to and from school, or act as an escort every time you go out. Often the effect of fear on others is denied because of the inability to cope with guilt. However, when the recognition occurs in conjunction with an honest appraisal of how fear is affecting you, and the motivation to do something about it, then it helps clear the way for progress.

Recognise the Long-term Effects of Fear

Learning to face up to and deal with fear is itself frightening, and fear of fear can be the greatest block to any kind of progress. It is essential, therefore, that you recognise, not only how fear is affecting you now, but also how it will damage your life in the long-term. Because fear leads to unprovoked attacks, excessive avoidance or unnecessary protection, it hinders, first and foremost, the ability to form healthy relationships. You cannot get close to people if you have an underlying fear of rejection, of being disliked or disapproved of, or being hurt in some other way, like being misunderstood, ridiculed, or having your most sensitive feelings trampled on. Ultimately this fear will lead to lack of friends and loneliness, and reduce the ability to function in a work setting. It is also the cause of many marital breakdowns.

Fear also reduces the possibility of personal success. For instance, fear can stop you from following your dreams: developing your talents, doing a college course, applying for the job you really want, seeking promotion.... And fear may prevent you from taking calculated risks, such as starting up your own business or moving house. It can, in fact, keep you from embarking on anything that involves change. You then become stuck in a rut, dissatisfied with life but unable to avail yourself of all that it has to offer. You could achieve so much more if fear didn't get in the way.

Fear affects every aspect of the self: emotional, spiritual, physical, mental. On the emotional front, fear may keep you from knowing yourself and being yourself, so you will be more likely to follow the crowd, to conform for the sake of conformity, and this leads to feelings of frustration, boredom and apathy. You will also find it more difficult to respond to beauty, to develop your aesthetic instincts and be in touch with the created world, so your soul will become impoverished. And in the spiritual realm, you may find it hard to open up to God's love, to know and trust God and discover the wealth of experience he has to offer. Fear also affects the body, keeping it from being healthy and attractive and making it vulnerable to disease. And it stunts the mind: the ability to think and reason, and be imaginative and creative – as the Creator intended.

When you shut down your feelings, refusing to face your fear or any other emotion, you also shut down part of your brain. This in turn makes it harder to think constructively and creatively, and you become more likely to be trapped by anxious and destructive thoughts. These thoughts can be so tenacious that you may come to believe that there really is no escape. However, since blocked-out thoughts or memories hinder the ability to learn and apprehend, it follows that facing the truth about yourself or any harmful experiences will release your cognitive potential. It will then be easier for you to assimilate the various methods of dealing with fear, beginning with some mental controls.

DEVELOP SOME MENTAL CONTROLS

Meditation

There are various thinking techniques that are useful for dealing with fear, and these are identical to those used in stress management: remember stress is a biochemical reaction that is triggered by fear. One of these is meditation, which is especially helpful for reducing anxiety. First take some deep breaths through the nose, exhaling slowly through the mouth. Then, imagine yourself in a scene that is particularly restful for you – lying on a beach with the waves lapping onto the shore; or in a garden with the scent of roses and the sound of bees; or perhaps sitting by a fire, the curtains drawn against the rain and cold. If you are not particularly imaginative, you may need to keep practicing this technique until you are able to hold the scene in your mind and keep the anxious thoughts from intruding. And remind yourself that, the more you get in touch with your blocked memories and feelings, the more capacity you will have to be imaginative.

You can also reduce your anxiety level by thinking about colours you find relaxing, or mentally quoting the Psalms or other Bible passages, or lines of poetry, or simply by taking time to enjoy the beauty of nature. The Bible tells us to fill our minds with things that are true, noble, right, pure, lovely, admirable, excellent and praiseworthy.[5] But first you have to experience such things; you cannot meditate on concepts and ideas you know nothing about. If you habitually fill your heart and mind with the good, true and beautiful, there will be no room for anxiety. Unfortunately, the reverse also is true, and if you are chronically anxious you may need, at the same time, to work at stopping the fearful thoughts, in order to make room for the positive ones.

Thought Stopping and Rehearsal

If you find yourself constantly thinking about things you might have said or done wrong, or some anticipated calamity, your thoughts going round and round in your head, you might find it helpful to try thought stopping. You can halt the mad whirl of anxious concerns by simply calling out, in your mind, the word, "Stop!" (If there is no one around, you can say it out loud!) This will cause your thoughts to jerk to a standstill, just long enough for you to set them off on a different track. You will probably have to keep practicing this technique until you are able to keep your thoughts from returning to their old, familiar round.

When your anxieties revolve around an actual future event, such as an interview, thought stopping is most useful when it is used in conjunction with a mental technique called rehearsal. With this you rehearse the entire scene in your mind, imagining the room and layout, picturing yourself walking in, sounding assured and confident, impressing your questioner, being offered the job.... Rehearsing stressful scenes in a positive manner will not only reduce the anxiety level, it will also make you more likely to succeed because you will be better prepared. You will also be more likely to view the situation in a rational manner.

Rational Controls

With chronic worry especially, developing some rational controls can be very effective. This involves asking yourself questions, such as, how likely is it that a feared event will actually happen? It might help to write down all the things you worried about last year or last month, or even last week, and then indicate which of them actually came to pass. Rational control also involves challenging your destructive thoughts with counter-arguments like, what is the evidence? Or, am I confusing a thought with a fact or focusing on irrelevancies? Am I thinking in all-or-nothing terms, taking things out of context or jumping to conclusions?

You might find it useful to contemplate how you would deal with a situation if you weren't worrying about it. It is surprising how less disturbing things are, and how easy to deal with, when fear doesn't get in the way. You can also apply rational controls by considering what effect a current situation will have in a week, a month, ten years! Anxiety becomes less of a problem when you can put things in perspective.

Mental Diversion

When the fear is not so much anxiety, but timidity, phobia or panic, then a method of controlling fear that is particularly effective is mental diversion. For example, if you are afraid of voicing your opinions in a group setting, have a fear of flying, or are afraid of having a panic attack while out shopping, you can alter the course of your thoughts by imagining yourself in the situation and coping with it. This differs from rehearsal in that it doesn't involve an actual forthcoming event.

Begin by relaxing your body, then imagine yourself facing your fear in easy stages. For example, if you have a social phobia, picture yourself walking through a door, seeing a few select friends with whom you feel safe, smiling and saying hello, chatting about mundane things.... Then gradually add some more people, perhaps one or two strangers, and see yourself starting a conversation about some more in-depth topic, voicing your opinions, being disagreed with, listening to their views and explaining your own. You can use this kind of mental imagery for any kind of frightening situation, taking your thoughts as far or as little as you want. Generally speaking, you are in control of your own thoughts. You can also learn to regulate your own body.

54

LEARN SOME MANAGEMENT SKILLS

Relaxation and Rest

Whatever the type of fear, but especially with chronic anxiety, it will help if you can develop the habit of relaxing generally, allowing your body to unwind and your mind to periodically switch off. Relaxation, which means becoming less rigid or tense, calms fear, reduces stress, and enables you to think more clearly and act more rationally. If you are permanently tense and find it difficult to calm down, you may first need to learn some relaxation techniques. One of these is quickie relaxation, which takes only a few minutes and can be carried out anywhere: at home, work, on the beach.... If appropriate, begin by loosening your clothes. Sit comfortably and close your eyes, while taking three deep breaths through the nose, exhaling slowly through the mouth. Then, breathing normally, stretch and tighten all your muscles. Then let your body go limp. Remain relaxed for about ten seconds, and finish with three more deep breaths.

Progressive relaxation takes longer: twenty to thirty minutes. And it is best carried out lying on a bed, again with your clothes loosened and your eyes closed. Following three deep breaths, curl up your toes, tightening all the muscles in your feet. Then let them relax. Now tighten and relax your calf muscles; then your thighs. Progress through all the major muscle groups in your body, ending with those in the face: around the jaw, eyes, forehead and scalp. The reason for tightening the muscles first is to enable them to relax more fully, just as pulling a pendulum far to the right will enable it to swing farther to the left.

You will find it generally beneficial if, as well as finding time to relax, you can also get into the habit of resting. This means abstaining from exertion or employment. Anxiety in particular can be triggered and exacerbated by the urge to keep going, often because of the compulsion to meet self-imposed deadlines. In order to be fully rested it is essential that you have enough sleep. Fear can seem overwhelming if you are chronically tired. It also means ensuring that you have time for the things you enjoy, such as reading, listening to music, pottering in the garden, walking by the sea or pursuing a hobby. Rest should be for the soul as well as the body, so also take time to just look around you and enjoy the beauty and wonder of creation. When you are able to rest, you will not only be better able to cope with fear, you will also find it easier to talk about it.

Communication

Talking is itself a way of coping with fear. Putting your fears into words provides a sense of relief; whereas fear, or any other emotion, that is bottled up grows until it becomes unbearable. Talking also enables you to see things differently and put your fears into perspective. It is especially releasing if your confidant is able to simply listen, without giving unsolicited advice, and is empathic and understanding. However, if you are anxious around people, are prone to timidity or have a social phobia, then the very thing you need to reduce fear may seem out of reach. In this case, the most constructive thing you can do is go back to basics and learn some communication skills. These revolve around the conveying and receiving of clear, unambiguous verbal messages that are not distorted by the thoughts and feelings of the sender or recipient.

As the speaker, or sender of a verbal message, your communication can be distorted by your perceptions of yourself or the person you are talking to. For instance, if you feel shy and think your opinions are stupid, then a supposedly confident message will come across as hesitant and unsure. Or if you are angry with the recipient, a neutral statement may sound harsh or aggressive. Your words can also be altered by thoughts and feelings about an unrelated past experience. If, for example, you have been ridiculed because of your ideas, then, consciously or unconsciously, you will be expecting the same response and your voice and general posture will change an assured pronouncement into a vague, uncertain one.

Whether or not your thoughts and feelings get in the way, your communication can become distorted through having the wrong body language; like saying, "I am not angry," with clenched hands. When the spoken and non-verbal messages don't agree, it is the body language that is the loudest. So, if you find yourself being constantly ignored or misunderstood, it might help to practice saying what you think or feel in front of a mirror. Whilst doing this, also take note of your style of speaking. Do you perhaps sound jocular when conveying hurt, or speak in a monotone when you really feel excited or angry? Observe also how you are with people. Do you use communication defences, such as interrupting, monopolising, moralising or jumping to conclusions? Do you react belligerently to constructive criticism or suggestions that are meant to be helpful? Or is it perhaps the language itself that you need to work on?

When it is the message itself that is distorted, through using incorrect, inadequate or ambiguous words, false grammar or wrong emphases, you might find it beneficial to listen to yourself on cassette. This can also improve your general delivery. If you have severe problems in this area, or if English is not your mother tongue, then you might want to enquire about classes at your local college. And don't let fear hold you back. It may be fear that has kept you from learning these basic skills in the first place.

Whilst working on your speaking abilities, you need to bear in mind that it might be the recipient who is distorting your message, because of his insecurities or preconceived ideas. If this happens frequently, then you can improve your communication skills by learning to listen. This will increase your awareness of how others may have misinterpreted your words, and enable you to work more effectively at increasing clarity and understanding. You can do this by asking for feedback: checking out and confirming that you have been heard correctly. However, in order to effectively complete any verbal transaction — the message being clearly given and received — you also need to be assertive.

Assertiveness

There are basically three ways of expressing your needs and opinions: you can be passive, aggressive or assertive. When your communication is passive, you may succeed in avoiding conflict but your needs will not be met, and you will not be respected. As a result you will be disappointed in yourself, and this will increase your anxiety in social situations. You are also likely to end up feeling angry and frustrated with others. Passive communication is characterised by such things as rambling statements or an excess of negatives. For example, "It's not really important, but would you...?" Your body language will reinforce your hesitancy through such things as slumped posture, shifting of weight, bowed head, downcast eyes, or apologetic, whiny or giggly tone.

If you are aggressive, you may get your needs met, or win an argument, but the other person will feel hurt and angry and may seek retaliation. So in the long run you will find yourself isolated and lonely, and this will reinforce any conviction that you are disliked, and increase your fear of people. Aggressive behaviour is characterised by such things as threats, accusations, put-downs and sarcasm; while your body will demonstrate aggression through stiff posture, clenched hands, finger pointing, glaring eyes, and angry or mocking voice.

When you are assertive, you are able to stand up for your rights but without violating the rights of others. With this type of behaviour you are more likely to achieve your goals. But whether or not you get what you want, you will feel confident, be able to respect yourself, and gain the respect of others. The topic of assertiveness is too detailed and comprehensive to address here. But if this is your particular problem area you may be able to find details of Assertiveness Training Courses through your GP or local college. In the meantime, you can practice being assertive by using clear, concise statements that are cooperative and understanding of the other's point of view, and by watching your body language. In order to appear confident, you need to stand firmly but relaxed on two feet, your hands loosely at your side; and use direct, but not staring, eye contact, have a pleasant expression and an assured tone of voice.

As you learn to communicate and be assertive, and are more relaxed and able to make time for rest, then you will be in a better position to overcome your fears, especially chronic anxiety, timidity or social phobia. But before you start making yourself go out and meet people, or try new skills, it might help to begin with some role-playing, assisted by a trusted partner or friend. For example, you can practice returning damaged merchandise, asking for a rise, or striking up a conversation with a stranger.

You may want to begin with a friendly stranger and progress to a shy or unsociable one. When you feel more confident with your role-playing, then you can start practicing for real. However, if your fears take the form of phobia or panic attacks, you will need to learn some additional skills, which involve facing and challenging the things you fear most.

CHALLENGE YOUR FEARS

Systematic Desensitisation

With any kind of phobia, the best way of dealing with the fear is to confront it, and the sooner the better. Unlike chronic anxiety or timidity, which are likely to have deep-rooted causes and require determination and patience to overcome, most phobias respond quickly to behavioural methods of treatment. If your fear is mild, or occurs only occasionally, you may be able to conquer it with help from your family or friends. If it is severely restricting your life, you may require some form of behavioural therapy. Usually, between six to ten sessions are all that are required, although this does not always eradicate the underlying feeling of anxiety. The two behavioural methods used to deal with fear related to specific stimuli are systematic desensitisation and rapid exposure.

Systematic desensitisation involves facing the feared entity in gradual stages and with a specific object in mind. For instance, if you are afraid of flying, your goal should be, "I want to fly to Paris for my holiday this year," rather than, "I want to lose my fear of flying." You commence by making a list of everything you find threatening about the thing or situation, from the least frightening to the most. Then you take steps to confront your fear, beginning at the easiest point.

At first you can do this in fantasy, facing the fear in your imagination. For example, if you are afraid of driving, and the least fearful thing is looking at the car, then you picture yourself just standing there, gazing at it. When you have got used to this, you imagine yourself approaching the car, opening the door, then sitting in the driver's seat. When this no longer provokes fear, you visualise yourself switching on the engine, putting the car in gear, releasing the handbrake, going through the routine checks and slowly moving away. You may then want to imagine yourself driving down a quiet country lane, then gradually merging with heavier traffic. If your phobia has resulted from an accident, you will end your fantasy by picturing the place where the accident occurred and manoeuvring safely through the black spot. The same principle applies for progressive desensitisation in actuality.

With some fears, you may only be able to confront them in your imagination, such as when the fear is of thunderstorms or of a bird or animal you see only rarely. But in these cases you may have access to slides or films that will enable you to view your fears on screen, using the same gradual methods of exposure. Or, you may be able to modify your reality. For instance, if you have a fear of birds which prevents you from going outside, you can begin by looking at pictures of birds, then face the reality in the form of a caged bird in the safety of a friend's home. First look at the caged bird from the other side of the room, then, as you are able to tolerate your feelings, move gradually closer. Then reach out and touch the bird. From here you will be able to take yourself outside and face the actuality you most dread: birds flying around in the open. With bird or animal phobias especially, it is helpful if a trusted family member or friend models positive responses to the feared object.

With many types of phobia, and with panic attacks, the support of family or friends is essential, and they must learn how to support your endeavours. For instance, with agoraphobia it is best to begin venturing out in company, and at first for short distances. Prior to setting out, you should determine on a fixed time to remain in the place you most fear and be prepared to ride out the panic. It might be useful to take some work project along, or a magazine, and sit and read until the panic passes and you can continue. With illness phobias, or obsessive-compulsive behaviour, your family should ignore your constant requests for reassurance so that you can learn to live with uncertainty or face up to the possibility of actually having the illness you dread. And they must give you positive reinforcement in the form of encouragement, praise or a small reward for every achievement.

Rapid Exposure

If you find the thought of gradual contact with the feared object daunting, you might do better with rapid exposure – also called Flooding or Implosive Therapy. This involves facing your fears head-on, without any build-up. It is rather like jumping in the deep end of a swimming pool when you can't swim. It might sound terrifying, but this method of challenging your fears can be very effective – and it's certainly quick. However, this is probably best done with a behavioural therapist who will stand by you, constantly reassuring you that you won't have a heart attack or suffer any physical or mental damage as a result of the confrontation. (If you have a known medical condition, then you would be better approaching your fears more gradually.) The therapist will also help you manage your feeling of fear, so that you can resist the urge to run from it.

With rapid exposure, as with systematic desensitisation, you can carry out the procedure in your imagination or in reality. For instance, if you are afraid of heights, you envisage yourself on the top of the tallest building you can think of, looking over a parapet to ant-like people hundreds of feet below. You stay with the picture until the nausea passes and you are able to feel calm and in control. A variation of this involves imagining the worst that can happen. This is often used as a defence, to avoid confronting what you are really afraid of. But when it is structured, being implemented for a set amount of time in the presence of a trusted friend to deal with a specific phobia, then it can have very positive results. While picturing the worst, and allowing yourself to feel the fear, you give a running commentary on your thoughts and feelings while your friend encourages you to hold onto your mental images for the time you have appointed. You will need to repeat the exercise until your reflections no longer evoke fear. In real life, you face your phobia by going with someone you trust directly to the place or situation you dread the most: a high building, crowded shopping centre or whatever. And you stay there until you no longer feel afraid.

A variation of rapid exposure is called paradoxical intention. For instance, if you fear having a heart attack, you try making your heart beat faster and actually bringing on an attack. You will soon prove to yourself that this is impossible, and so lose your fear. Paradoxical intention is sometimes effective for insomnia. You tell yourself that you mustn't go to sleep and try your hardest to remain awake. You will find, paradoxically, that you can't keep your eyes open.

Whatever method you use to face your fear, you need also to watch how you talk to yourself. It is essential that you constantly encourage yourself, and that when you succeed you reward yourself, perhaps with some small treat, but certainly with a spontaneous and pleased, "Well done!" You also need to be patient with yourself. Don't berate yourself because of any setbacks or failures. These are inevitable. However, if none of the mental controls or coping methods have any lasting effect, then perhaps your fears are more deep-rooted, arising from hurts and traumas that have never been dealt with. In this case, it is necessary to go back into the past, recognise and work through the pain, and find healing and release. Only then can you start growing beyond fear into the calmness of faith.

5

GROWING BEYOND FEAR

REMOVE THE HINDRANCES

Recognise Past Trauma

Life is all about growth and development. However old we
are, we should continue to grow in wisdom and understanding,
and become increasingly more aware of all aspects of our inner
selves and more able to fulfil our potential. But often growth is
halted or slowed down because of unresolved hurt or trauma.
Therefore, in order to grow beyond fear into faith, it is necessary
to deal with those emotional blocks that keep us stuck in a pattern
of recurring anxiety. This is especially indicated when the fear
has no specific object, being experienced as a nameless dread or a
vague sense of impending doom. But before the hindrances can
be removed, they have to be recognised and identified.

The obstacles to growth, as discussed in Chapter 2,
may consist of unprocessed emotional pain arising from an
especially traumatic incident, such as a bereavement, accident or
environmental disaster; or from ongoing abuse of any kind. With
the last, the most damage occurs when the abusers have been
parents or other carers. Hindrances can also arise because of
emotional harm caused by such things as bullying and teasing,
rejection, ridicule or constant criticism.

You may not, until now, have recognised the trauma
because it was so painful and frightening that you blotted it from
memory. Or you may have discounted or minimised it: "It wasn't
all that bad." On the other hand, you may not have noticed
psychological damage because of its gradual build-up, or because
the trauma was cushioned by a supportive family environment.
But even if your parents were basically loving and accepting,
their own struggles with depression, stress, low self-esteem or
some domestic problem may have prevented them from giving

63

you the confidence in yourself that is vital for healthy emotional development.

If, on the whole, your childhood was a happy one, you may be surprised and dismayed at any realisation that you have developed a propensity to fear because of a parent's failure in some area. But you must face the truth, however painful this is, not in order to allocate blame or create conflict, but with the purpose of recognising and removing the hindrances to growth. At the same time, it will help if you can see their failings in the larger context of their general conduct and motives. If your family was very dysfunctional, you may not be able to find much that was positive about your upbringing; but generally parents want to do their best for their children, and any damage caused is unintentional. Moreover, the harm only persists into adulthood if it was part of an ongoing pattern, such as parents consistently putting a child down, or repeatedly failing to recognise its unique strengths and abilities. If you are a parent yourself, you needn't be concerned that any failings on your part will irrevocably damage your child. Children are very resilient, and as long as they generally feel loved and safe they are not going to be harmed by their parents being human and not always getting it right.

In order to locate and identify your own emotional impediments, and incidentally be better able to facilitate growth in others, you will have to take a mental trip back into your past, honestly recalling the true facts. You can do this in several ways. You may want to begin by actively thinking about the main events in your life, in chronological order, perhaps making notes in a journal or writing it all down in story form. Or you may prefer to browse through photograph albums and stir up your memory in this manner. Another, often more effective, method is to simply let your mind wander, while you're in the bath or having a coffee break, and start connecting events, places, and things said to you by various people at different times. However you choose to go about it, you will eventually build up a picture of your life, with its mixture of happy memories and not so happy ones. And the more clearly you can discern the original causes of your fear, the easier it will be to also recognise fear itself, even when it is camouflaged.

Remove the Disguises

It has been noted that fear is often disguised as anger. So, if you have a short fuse or tend to seethe inwardly, and you have never been able to maintain control over your anger, then ask yourself if you are, in fact, dealing with the wrong problem. Maybe the predominant feeling is a deep anxiety that you have been reluctant to acknowledge because of the additional fear that comes from feeling weak or helpless. Or maybe you are displacing fear, in the form of anger, onto the wrong person because this is less threatening that admitting whom you are really afraid of. True strength and control comes from facing the reality, no matter how disturbing, and doing something about it. Paradoxically, it takes courage to admit that you are afraid.

Fear may also be disguised as bravado or rash acts of bravery. In this case, what seems like courage is actually an attempt, conscious or otherwise, to cover up the true feeling underneath. Ask yourself, therefore, if you try to promote a tough-guy image, clown around to hide insecurity, or talk a lot to conceal an underlying nervousness? Or do you perhaps engage in dangerous sports or have a job that places you in physical danger? Enjoying challenge and danger is not in itself an indication of unrecognised fear. But if you tend to take unnecessary risks it would be well to ask yourself if, rather than being immune from fear, or being able to subdue it, you are actually trying to avoid it.

It might also be helpful to question any tendency to low mood, or propensity to tension or unease, as fear is one of the causes of depression and the trigger for stress. Maybe the feelings of despondency or oppression are themselves cover-ups, these disguises being socially more acceptable and personally less threatening – however debilitating. If you suspect that fear is a factor, then taking more notice of your feelings and pondering the origins of your proneness to depression or stress will enable you to start removing this particular concealment. And, incidentally, it will also begin lifting your mood and easing any sense of strain.

When disturbed feelings or mood swings are connected with the ups and downs of a stormy relationship, then fear might be parading in the guise of love. This camouflage is the most difficult to penetrate, but you can begin by pondering the question, what is love? There are different kinds of love, but if you understand it to consist of knowledge, respect, responsibility and care, then you can use these as markers to indicate if what you have is the genuine article. Do you, for instance, really know and respect your partner, and is your feeling of responsibility guided by knowledge and respect? Do you care about the other's needs, and about meeting those needs? And how about your partner's professions of love for you? If you are constantly being hurt, then you may be staying partly because of self-deception; also because of a long habit of ignoring emotional pain.

Work through the Pain

In order to find healing from deep emotional wounds, and so be better prepared to deal with current hurts, you have to let your feelings come to the surface. You can start the process by talking about difficult aspects of your life to someone you trust. The more you talk about painful happenings, the more you will feel the associated feelings and be able to release them, usually through tears or constructive anger. Prayer too is a helpful outlet for pent-up emotions, but only when you are truthful, and willing also to listen to God, allowing him to direct you to caring, listening people. If prayer is used as a means of self-deception, to avoid facing your true sentiments or talking to others about them, then it is counterproductive. If you cannot immediately find someone to talk to, then writing a journal might help. Or perhaps you would prefer to express your pain and confusion through art or music.

As you begin to release the pain, you must ensure that you don't keep re-infecting old wounds through putting yourself down, telling yourself, for instance, that you are stupid or incompetent, or that you were born anxious or timid and will never be any different. Some people are naturally loud and extrovert, others are quiet and reflective, and you should not try to change what is essentially you. Loudness does not equal confidence, and quietness is not the same as timidity. Watch, therefore, how you talk to yourself and, as you would with physical wounds, treat your damaged soul with gentleness and care.

Your wounded soul can only be fully healed as, having cleaned and protected it, you then let go of the emotional pain. This is the essence of forgiveness. However, in order to forgive, you first have to work through the pain; short-circuiting the process will leave you with a deep well of anguish that will periodically burst to the surface, revealing itself in bouts of anger, depression, stress, or surges of fear. Forgiving someone doesn't mean that you accept what has been done to you. On the contrary! Forgiveness is for something that is unacceptable. Neither does it mean justifying or excusing any mistreatment, or continuing to tolerate it. To forgive means facing the full extent of the harm done to you, letting go of the need for revenge or restitution, and moving on.

If you have been abused, or sense that you may be repressing some traumatic event, then you may need professional help to recover and deal with past traumas, work through the pain and facilitate growth. While behavioural therapy can be very effective in helping you overcome a specific phobia or cope with panic attacks, when fear is deep rooted a more analytical form of treatment is indicated. Psychotherapists and psychodynamic counsellors in particular have been trained to help you explore in a safe environment any past issues that are continuing to cause pain and hinder development. They will also help you get in touch with and identify blocked feelings so that you can become more fully alive. But whether or not you decide to avail yourself of professional assistance, you can work at promoting your own growth and development through enhancing self-esteem.

DEVELOP A HEALTHY SENSE OF SELF

Strengthen your Self-Identity

Any abnormal exposure to fear, especially that occurring in childhood, damages self-esteem, which in turn increases the propensity to fear. It is a downward spiral. Frightening incidents, traumatic accidents, natural disasters and the like create feelings of confusion and helplessness; and with abuse there is also shame, guilt, and a sense of worthlessness. All these impair one's innate sense of self as lovable, valuable and changeable. But perhaps more disturbingly, they destroy the inherent knowledge of oneself as a unique individual with a specific place in the universe and a designated purpose. It is this erosion of self-identity that gives rise to the vague feelings of nameless dread or fearful foreboding that often typify chronic anxiety, and that sometimes underlie the other forms of fear.

Nowadays, people tend to base their identity primarily on their roles. For example, I am a doctor (work role), or I am a mother (relationship role). So, when this role is taken away, for whatever reason – retirement, being made redundant, marriage break-up, children leaving home – the sense of self is seriously impaired. However, our identity is based also on such things as our gender, personal traits, beliefs and values, interests and goals. And as well as being formed by our personal attributes, we have also been shaped by our families and the environment as a whole. Therefore, the more you know about yourself, your family, your national socio-political history, and your religious and cultural heritage, the more clearly defined will be your picture of yourself.

Our identity is not like a photograph, fixed in time. We are what we were, what we are, and what we hope to become. Like our outward appearance, it changes as we get older and circumstances alter, as we acquire new knowledge and modify our views and opinions. But deep inside there is an essential self that is unchanging and eternal. And if you are going to be able to stand firm, with a deep sense of calm, when you hear and read of frightening and threatening situations in your own family and the world at large, then you also have to be in touch with this primitive, intangible part of your being.

The essential self is basically spiritual, which in its wider sense incorporates our innate sense of the aesthetic and our natural urge to create. More specifically, it is a shared knowledge of the divine, of having been created in God's image and entrusted with a privileged role as stewards responsible for the well-being of the entire created world. When you are able to develop a sense of identity that is based not only on your place and role in the temporal world, but also on your existence in God, then you will have a very stable foundation on which to develop a healthy concept of yourself.

Improve your Self-Concept

Self-concept is how you perceive yourself, and if your life has been dogged by chronic fear then you are likely to view yourself in a negative light, seeing only the less acceptable parts of your character. You may even have reinforced a negative view by focusing on your fears, telling yourself that you are a coward or scaredy-cat, or that you are weak or inadequate and can't cope like other people. However, a healthy self-concept means that you see yourself as you really are, recognising your strengths and abilities as well as your weaknesses. When you have a realistic view of yourself you will be neither inflated by your positive attributes nor cast down by the negative ones. And you will be able to work more effectively at becoming the person you really want to be.

In order to develop your full potential you must first get rid of the old voices from the past, telling you perhaps that you are ugly, stupid, no good, or will never amount to anything. You need also to be wary about being too dependent on the opinions of others. When self-esteem has been damaged in the formative years there is a strong need for reassurance. But, if fear has kept you from forming healthy relationships or succeeding in the workplace, then others' opinions are more likely to reinforce an already negative view of yourself. They may, for instance, think you have no opinions worth listening to because you come across as hesitant and unsure, or regard you as not very bright because fear has prevented you from making full use of your cognitive abilities. While it can be very reaffirming to have positive feedback from friends and work colleagues, your view of yourself must essentially be your own. Deep down, you know the kind of person you really are, and what you are capable of achieving.

At the most basic level, how we view ourselves is linked with our concept of how God sees us. And since we have an innate sense of the divine, this occurs whether or not there is any conscious acknowledgement of God's existence. As our Creator, God sees us as essentially good and valuable: a creator is always proud of a well-made creation. And although we have become tarnished by sin and our bodies ravaged by time, the fundamental goodness remains. Just as a valued painting can become spoiled by the dirt and dust of centuries, and the amateur attempts to repair the damage, underneath there is still a masterpiece. Maybe fear has prevented you from living life to the full, but if you can recognise your essential goodness and start tapping into your innate creative ability, then you will be well on the way to developing a healthy self-esteem.

Enhance your Self-Esteem

Acquiring healthy self-esteem involves more than being confident and learning how to relate. It means developing every aspect of the self: heart, mind, body, soul and spirit. It also means recognising and humbly acknowledging your place and role in the universe, as well as your unique strengths and abilities. As self-esteem improves, you will have less need to hide behind your defences because any distorted views of yourself, others and God will be diminished. And with a deepening sense of emotional security, you will be able to look inside yourself without trepidation, confidently face the world, and come to God in prayer, assured of your welcome at all times.

The Bible teaches that perfect love casts out fear. And on this basis, the best place to start improving self-esteem is with the social self, or heart: that part of a human that is concerned with the receiving and giving of love. When self-esteem is low, and especially when it is marked by fear, there is a tendency to see ourselves as unlovable and not worth knowing, and to reject others before they have a chance to reject us. If this is you, then you can reverse this trend by opening yourself up to others, allowing them to show care and affection, compliments, praise, and offers of practical help. Above all, start accepting the love that God is longing to show you. The more you receive love, from other people and God, the more you will have to give, and the less fearful you will be of giving.

As well as enlarging your heart, you also need to improve your mind: the thinking part of the self. First, accept that God has given you a brain and that he means you to use it. Then, work at stimulating your natural curiosity and sense of wonder, perhaps by opening your eyes to the beauty of nature, by reading, or pursuing a long-dormant interest. As you do this, you will find yourself increasingly asking questions and wanting to check out, test, prove and discover. Eventually, your urge to explore and experience new things will override the fears that, until now, have kept you from developing your true cognitive potential.

The same principles apply with physical enhancement. The more you value and respect your own body, the more you will want to take care of it, through having a healthy, well-balanced diet, sufficient rest and exercise. You will also find yourself paying greater attention to your appearance and, as a result, becoming increasingly aware of its more positive aspects. As your body image improves, you will then be less afraid of others' imagined dislike or derision, and you will stop hiding away.

It is especially important that you work at enhancing your soul, which can be defined as the sensing self. It is that part of a human concerned with life, feelings and creative thought. If your life is crammed with a hundred and one worries, then the soul, the source of life, shrivels up and dies. But as you nurture it, through allowing it time and space for quietness and reflection and exposing it to beauty and goodness, then you will find more enjoyment in simply being. You will experience a wider range of emotions, and creative thoughts and ideas will germinate and flourish — so there will be no room for fear.

The soul is, in some respects, inseparable from the spirit; that part of a human that tends him towards God and enables him to commune with God. A healthy self-esteem cannot develop if the focus is only on the visible aspects of the self. The spiritual too is essential. But, when life has been dominated by fear because of past abuse or trauma, there is a tendency to view God in a negative light, rather than seeing him as he truly is. Fear of God should be in the form of awe and wonder, not terror and dread. If you are having difficulty in this area, begin by simply opening your mind to the possibility of there being something more wonderful and exciting than you have ever realised. Then start praying – it doesn't matter what words you use – read the Bible, beginning with the Gospels, and find a church where you feel comfortable and at home. With this, as with the enrichment of every other aspect of the self, you need to develop at your own speed and in your own way.

The topic of self-esteem is wide-ranging, and is addressed more fully in the book by this author, *Self-esteem: The way of humility*. Suffice it here to reiterate that developing a firm sense of identity, having a realistic self-concept and a healthy regard for every part of the self is vital if, rather than merely learning how to cope with fear, you are able to grow beyond it.

CULTIVATE FAITH

Trust Yourself

Whatever form your particular fear takes – anxiety, timidity, phobia or panic – your fear can be turned into faith. And the first person you need to believe in is yourself. The ability to trust your own motives and feelings, thoughts, ideas and judgements increases with the development of a healthy self-esteem. As already indicated, this is not a false boosting of the ego, but a realistic assessment of your strengths and abilities as well as your failures and weaknesses. This honest self-appraisal is only possible as you get to know yourself, and you do this by looking inward, from the perspective of a solid external viewpoint, asking yourself what you are feeling in any given situation, reflecting on your interests, wondering about your opinions. Are they really your own, or are you merely echoing someone else's? Do you have sufficient facts to form an opinion? And do you feel secure enough to be flexible, to listen to other people's beliefs, assess them, perhaps incorporate them into your own, modifying, changing...? It is only when you have convictions that are truly your own that you can develop an unwavering faith in yourself.

Believing yourself means also trusting your own instincts. When fear becomes pervasive, this intuitive ability is lost, resulting in a general feeling of uncertainty. You wonder if it really is safe to get close to your partner, open up to a friend, attempt a new skill, visit a new place.... Again, this ability is restored and developed as you get to know yourself. So start taking notice of your impressions when you are with your partner or friend, tune into your gut feelings when you meet someone for the first time, be aware of your sensations when you are in new surroundings. And then start trusting your instincts, which are really just an accumulation of unconsciously stored observations and comparisons. At the same time, have faith in your ability to learn new skills, accomplish new feats, succeed in new ventures. You will, of course, make mistakes. Who doesn't? There will be times when you misjudge a person or situation and get hurt. But when you have sufficient faith in yourself you will be able to learn from your mistakes and move on, instead of letting fear flare up again, sending you back behind your defences.

Learn to Trust Others

As well as trusting yourself, you also need to develop a belief in other human beings. Trust is the very first thing a baby learns. It forms the basis for progression through the various developmental stages in a child's life, such as learning to be independent. So if trust has been betrayed from the start, by the very people you were dependent on for your emotional and physical needs, then it is especially difficult to form secure relationships later on. It is also hard to trust again if you have been mistreated in any way, or let down by a spouse, partner or close friend. This is because there is a tendency to see large sections of humanity as being like your betrayers. However, you can begin to lose this unhealthy fear by reminding yourself that you have transferred onto others the characteristics or behaviours of those who have hurt you. Then, just as it is necessary to know yourself in order to trust yourself, you need to develop sufficient knowledge of others before you can, with impunity, place your trust in them.

In order to know others, you will first need to start undoing the effects of unhealthy fear. That is, you must stop attacking people, whether physically or emotionally, and stop avoiding them or putting up unnecessary defences. Instead, make an effort to go where people are. Join a church or club, go to evening classes, take up a sport.... As with everything else, you will need to pace yourself. You know how fast you can go. And remind yourself that it is unrealistic to expect to be able to trust everyone to the same extent. If you are emotionally healthy, you will have a wide circle of acquaintances, a group of friends to socialise with, and a few close friends in whom you can safely confide.

When trust has been betrayed, it is especially hard to trust others with your innermost feelings. Trust can only be learned as another proves himself trustworthy, so you will need time to put your confidant to the test. But it will be well worth the effort and risk involved. As you feel safer you will discover the healing that comes from knowing you can bare your soul to another person, secure in the knowledge that your deepest and most sacred thoughts, ideas and feelings will not be trampled on with insensitive remarks or misunderstanding. This same principle of restoration applies also to God.

Start Trusting God

With God, as with other people, you can only learn to trust, and thereby find healing from past hurts, as you allow him the opportunity to prove himself trustworthy. We are told that faith comes from hearing, and hearing from God's Word.[6] In other words, we learn to trust God as we get to know him, which, as the Bible terms it, is to know the unknowable. Faith in God should not be blind, any more than faith in people should be indiscriminate. Rather, we are meant to have a reason for our faith. Our grounds for believing are based partly on rational knowledge, and this comes from studying God's Word as it is revealed in Scripture, and through his works in creation. We also get to know God through the example of godly men and women;

74

those who, within the limitations of their human make-up, reflect God's character and ways of working with people. We also get to know God through personal experience. Many times in Scripture we are challenged to prove God, to put him to the test and discover that he is there, that he does answer prayer and that he does bring order and meaning to our lives. The more you understand God and experience him for yourself, the more you will be able to believe; and the more you can put your trust in his goodness and power, the less reason you will have to be afraid.

Maybe you have been told by a well-meaning Christian that if only you trusted God you wouldn't feel afraid – or be depressed or stressed or feel overwhelmed by life. But if you have been hurt by another human, and have perhaps felt that God doesn't listen or care, then you have to go back to the beginning, like a newborn baby with a loving and nurturing parent, and learn to trust all over again. A parent soothes a child's fear, not with a demand that the child have faith, but with the reassurance that Mum or Dad is there. Perhaps you have tried to stop being afraid so that you can be more trusting. But it actually works the other way round. Discovering that someone else – human or divine – can be trusted makes you feel protected and safe. And this provides a solid foundation on which you can grow, as children grow, beyond fear into an ever-deepening faith.

Hold on to Trust

It is human to fear, and there are times when it is wise to be afraid. But because, nowadays, there is so much exposure to threatening and frightening situations, it is becoming increasingly difficult to develop and hold on to faith. Ultimately, all fear – whether it takes the form of anxiety, timidity, phobia or panic – is fear of the unknown. It follows, then, that increased knowledge will result in a reduction of fear. This includes knowledge of fear itself, its signs and symptoms, causes and effects, and knowledge of how fear can be managed.

However, in order to truly grow beyond fear, factual knowledge is not enough. You need to know, or be acquainted with, yourself, other people and God; and through that knowledge learn to esteem and trust the beautiful and good. Only then will you have a deep, inner sense of safety and calm, which is the antithesis of fear, even when you are confronted with the many things in life that are too big to grasp and understand. Faith is not founded on nothing; it is based on the knowledge that someone is there, within us, around us, at our side, to hold and comfort us, keeping us safe. Faith is the assurance that, however alarming things seem, it will be alright.

Coping skills can be learned fairly quickly. But growth, in any area, is a life-long process. You can begin now by removing the hindrances to psychological and spiritual development and stepping out, beyond fear, into the light and life of faith.

Endnotes

1   1 Samuel 18.7
2   1 John 4.18
3   1 Corinthians 16.10-11
4   Philippians 2.20
5   Philippians 4.8
6   Romans 10.17

Silvertree Grobooks

Jennifer Minney

Beyond depression: Growing into light
ISBN: 0-9538446-3-3

Beyond fear: Growing into faith
ISBN: 0-9538446-5-X

Beyond stress: Growing into serenity
ISBN: 0-9538446-4-1

Using Bible characters as case studies, each book discusses signs and symptoms, current triggers and deep-rooted causes, and provides guidelines for overcoming the immediate effects. The emotional difficulties are also viewed in the context of the entire person, and the reader is helped to find healing from past traumas and begin changing destructive patterns of thinking and behaviour; to move beyond the problem towards spiritual and psychological wholeness.

All titles £3.50

Coming soon:

Beyond anger: Growing into calm
Beyond marital discord: Growing into love
Beyond parenting chaos: Growing into harmony

Also by Jennifer Minney

Self-esteem: The way of humility

This thoughtful book promotes the development of self-esteem on the basis of one's identity in God, through creation and redemption. This foundation, it explains, is essential for creating a respect for self that is humble and grateful, and that leads to a more responsible and effective stewardship of one's gifts and abilities.

The author, a counsellor with a BA (Hons) in Psychology, and more than twenty years experience of helping people with low self-esteem, draws also on her Bible college, nursing and midwifery training to explore and discuss five aspects of the self: body, soul, spirit, heart and mind. With each, there is a survey of common misconceptions and problems, with guidelines for overcoming them.

£5.95   **ISBN: 0-9538446-2-5**

Will Jesus kick my ball back?

The amazing story of an adoption that should have been impossible, of cerebral palsy, and a child whose avid curiosity and irrepressible giggles have made him a joy to many.

It is also the story of the author's spiritual and psychological journey, from a background of abuse and rejection, through years of infertility, to a place of trust in God's goodness, even when his long-promised child turns out to be severely brain-damaged. It is a story of learning to open up to God's love and experiencing him, no longer as rigid and punitive, but as a loving, approachable Father with whom it is safe to be oneself, to be child-like — to play.

The two stories blend as mother and child grow together, developing their full potential as she learns to love herself and a child whom a neurologist had written off.

This book has had a profound impact on those who have read it, provoking laughter, producing tears, challenging, uplifting and enriching the soul. It is a book that is hard to put down.

£6.95   **ISBN: 0-9538446-0-9**

All Silvertree titles are available from bookshops or can be purchased (postage free in UK) direct from:

Silvertree Publishing
PO Box 2768
Yeovil
Somerset BA22 8XZ

Become a Silvertree Book Agent

If you found this book helpful, why not become a Silvertree Book Agent, and so benefit others whilst also earning money for yourself, your church, or your favourite charity?

For full details, send an s.a.e. to the above address.